The Right Reverend William J. McDonald

Monsignor McDonald, Rector of The Catholic University of America since 1957, is a priest of the Archdiocese of San Francisco and former Director of Newman Clubs at Stanford University and San Francisco State College. Author and contributor to periodicals, he was Associate Editor of the *Monitor,* official organ of the Archdiocese of San Francisco, and of the scholarly journal, *The New Scholasticism.* Since being awarded his Ph.D. degree he has been given many honorary degrees from universities in the United States and abroad. His latest recognition came with his election as President of the worldwide Federation of Catholic Universities.

THE GENERAL COUNCIL

Special Studies in Doctrinal and
Historical Background

Edited and with a foreword by
Rt. Rev. Msgr. William J. McDonald

The Catholic University of America Press
Washington D.C.
1962

Nihil obstat:

Clement V. Bastnagel
Censor Deputatus

Imprimatur:

Patrick A. O'Boyle, D.D.
Archbishop of Washington
July 25, 1962

The *nihil obstat* and *imprimatur* are official declarations that a book or pamphlet is free of doctrinal or moral error. No implication is contained therein that those who have granted the *nihil obstat* and the *imprimatur* agree with the content, opinions, or statements expressed.

Printed in the United States of America
Library of Congress Catalog Card Number: 62-20329

Dedicated to the Memory

of

Father Edmond D. Benard

ZEALOUS PRIEST, SKILLED THEOLOGIAN,
ELOQUENT PREACHER,
AND CULTURED GENTLEMAN

Contents

Foreword

I f, as the spanish thinker Donoso Cortes has observed, every great question is ultimately a theological one, then the decisions of the councils of the Church must lie at the very heart of history. Even though unaware of such decisions, men are inevitably influenced by them. Of widespread interest, therefore, should be an endeavor to supply background information and to recreate history in the work of some of the great councils. Such is the purpose of this volume.

The chapters appearing here were first presented by their scholarly authors as lectures in a planned series at The Catholic University of America. Nearly a century has elapsed since the last General Council was convened; hence the understandable vagueness in the minds of many as to its precise nature and mode of operation. In accordance with the wish of His Holiness, Pope John XXIII, who urged that every means should be employed to bring about a better knowledge of the aims and work of the Council, it was appropriate that the lecture series, open to the public, should be sponsored by our National Pontifical University.

It was felt, also, that the series would not serve its purpose best by a mere recounting of historical and other aspects of all of the general councils. Rather the aim should be to make "come alive," as it were, a selected few dealing with pivotal problems and exercising a special impact on the peoples of their day and of subsequent ages. Thus it would be possible to observe the formation of great theological decisions as they were forged in the friction of earnest discussion. One could watch, so to speak, as the true notion of the nature of Christ was carefully brought into focus at the First Council of Nicea or participate in the enthusiasm of the populace at Ephesus after the proclamation of the doctrine of Mary's divine maternity. In this way history would be re-vitalized and would vibrate in these important dramas of the ages.

While all this should help to provide a setting, nevertheless the Second Vatican Council seems unique in at least one respect. Others were convoked as a result of the insistent tolling of some major crisis in the long history of the Church, be it growing heresy or rending schism. The latest Council has a more positive aim which is beautifully summarized by our Holy Father in his address at the closing session of one of the preparatory commissions:

> To put it briefly but completely, it is the aim of the council that the clergy should acquire a new brilliance of sanctity, that the people be instructed efficaciously in the truths of the Faith and Christian morals, that the new generations, who are growing like a hope of better times, should be educated properly; that attention be given to the social apostolate and that Christians should have a missionary heart, that is to say, brotherly and friendly toward all and with all.

Finally, I wish to take this occasion to express sincere gratitude to the eminent scholars who have given so generously of their time and talents to present these perceptive studies, studies made possible under the Monsignor George A. Dougherty Foundation and a generous gift from Monsignor Donald A. MacLean. To the late Father Edmond D. Benard, who was of particular help in the planning stages, this book is dedicated. May it be a worthy memorial of a truly noble and cultured priest.

Rt. Rev. Msgr. William J. McDonald, Rector
The Catholic University of America

February 2, 1962.

The General Council
in the Teaching of the Church

The General Council
in the Teaching of the Church

FOR THE CATHOLIC, the abiding reality that determines his whole relation to the living God is the fact that he is a member of the Body of Christ. This fact in turn takes its rise from the two elements that constitute historical Christianity itself; namely, the Incarnation and the Church. For by reason of the Incarnation the power of God unto salvation visibly and effectively entered into human history. Through Jesus Christ, God not only illumines the minds of men but works to transform human nature and make it to share in the divine life which Christ came to give. However, man's participation in this new life, this new spiritual order, inaugurated by the Incarnate Word is, by divine institution, to take place in a community, a visible society of men and women. In this society alone will Christ find His fulness. It is this society, His Church, founded by Him and vitally united to Him as branches to the vine, that Christ uses to extend His redemptive work to every age. It is through the Church, His Body, that Christ will gradually form that new humanity of which He is the first born of many brethren. Hence it is that only in the context of this vital relation between Christ and His Church does the Catholic find the full meaning of his Catholic faith and life. For just as God's redemptive love for mankind bodies forth and accomplishes its purposes through the visible, historical instrument of a human nature conjoined to the Person of the Word, so also with the Church. By the will of God not only the truth and grace of Christ in its fulness but Christ Himself continue to enter into the history of man by means of a visible, historical instrument, that is, a society, so vitally united to Christ Himself that St. Paul describes it as His Body, the Church. It is this Body united to its Head, Christ, that throughout history unites the divine and the human, the eternal and the temporal into a faithful image and living extension of the Incarnation.

Yet while emphasizing this sacramental character of the Church, it is not to be maintained that it is a perfect image. Such perfection will come only at the end of history itself when God shall be "all in all." Until that moment, which lies in the unsearchable judgment of God, the work of Christ is incomplete and unfinished. Christ, therefore, by means of His Body, the Church, will work in and through the history of humanity until the eternal design of God is complete. Indeed, it is this interaction between God's design and the historical process (to which the very existence of the Church bears witness) that is the key to the Catholic understanding of the history of the Church itself. Thus the historical manifestations and developments of papal authority, of hierarchical governance, of legislative direction, of educational activity, of missionary zeal; all these, to the eyes of faith, are manifestations of the continuous interactions, in the Church, of God's design and the historical process. But it seems to me that nothing so graphically mirrors this interaction as does a general council. For here in dramatic form and on a vivid canvas are found all the elements that enter into this interaction: revealed truth, the guidance of the Holy Spirit, divine authority delegated to men. There is a whole congeries of circumstances and events that gradually lead up to the council. Present are the virtues and passions that enter into the actions of free agents: ambition, envy, pursuit of power, but also sanctity, wisdom, prudence, fortitude. There is the clash of ideas and personalities, party spirit, political maneuvering either subtly or openly self-seeking. Yet through it all there is a consciousness of God working through the very density of history until that moment when the decision is given in words similar to those of St. Peter, addressing the Council at Jerusalem, "It has seemed good to the Holy Spirit and to us."[1] Looked at from this point of view, each of the councils, in its

---

[1] Acts 15:28.

own way, seems to constitute a point at which the torrent of history appears to pause and for a passing instant to crystallize and be immobile. At that moment you can sense, though not fully understand, how God has used human history and human passion and human error to make His truth shine all the more brightly.

As an illustration of this interaction furnished by the general councils, I should like to take the first Ecumenical Council of Nicea. At issue is the central truth of Christianity itself, the divinity of Christ. Believed and affirmed in the Church from the beginning, witnessed to in her liturgical life and catechetical instruction, still this truth must be explained and developed for the Greco-Roman world in which it was being preached, a world in which cultured minds were deeply colored by oriental religious ideas and Greek philosophy. In this intellectual milieu the truth of Christ's divinity must be so formulated that men's desire for understanding be satisfied and yet not the truth itself, emptied of mystery, degenerate into mere rationalism. The reality must be so expressed that the meaning of the scriptures is clearly retained, yet not allow scriptural phrases to be legitimately employed to sustain any form of subordinationism. To be able, therefore, so to theologize and explain this truth for the educated catechumen and defend it from misunderstanding, the Christian teachers had to take concepts and terms from the culture in which they lived and adapt them to their theological needs. In such a situation the development of a common usage and understanding of concepts is a slow process. While it is in process there will be inconsistencies, hesitancies, false emphases, as well as distortions. Accordingly, controversies develop, heresies arise, common efforts are undertaken on a local level to deal with problems, until finally the controversy and the uncertainty are so widespread that they demand that an authoritative judgment "erect a witness to the truth" for the whole Church to see.

A doctrinal issue such as this, however, is not settled in the abstract, nor does the process of its resolution transcend the human element which is necessarily an integral part of any council. As is ever the case in human affairs, there are intermingled both human personalities and historical events. So we have

Arius, well educated but strongly rationalistic. He was a per-
sonable man but driven by pride and ambition and, by every
evidence, committed to heterodox opinions for a long time.[2] An
able and well trained dialectician, he uses his dialetical skill to
throw into strong relief the difficulties of the Catholic doctrine
and to avoid formulating any integral position of his own. In
the beginning, too, he is aided by the misplaced tolerance of
Alexander, the Bishop of Alexandria, whom Arius accuses publicly of Sabellianism. Only reluctantly does Alexander move
against Arius, and by that time the doctrine of Arius is widespread and Arius himself has secured powerful support at the
imperial court. For it is at this very point in history that the civil
power begins to play a decisive part in the affairs of the Church.
Constantine had publicly recognized the Church, seeing in it not
only a source of religious vitality but an instrument for peace
and concord in the empire. He is convinced that in serving these
ends he is also serving the best interests of the Church, and so for
him a doctrinal controversy by its very nature has political dimen-
sions. It is this same political dimension that creates a new figure
in the life of the Church, the so-called court bishop, one akin to
Eusebius of Nicomedia, the chief supporter of Arius and a fore-
most adviser of Constantine. These men are not deeply interested
in what is orthodox or heterodox; their primary concern is power
and its exercise, and their ambition will taint this whole situation
for the next century.

It is this welter of personalities and passion and conflict and
spreading division that draws Constantine personally into the
situation. In the beginning he is badly informed, and he sees the
whole thing as "a worthless and insignificant quarrel" and feels
that brothers are opposing brothers "for the sake of trifles."[3] In
this tone he sends to both Arius and Alexander a letter which is
delivered to them by Ossius of Cordoba. After his first hand experience, Ossius seems to have convinced Constantine of the
seriousness of the situation and the need for a widely representative body to settle it.[4] The result is that Constantine con-

[2] Cf. Hefele-Leclercq, *Histoires des Conciles* T. 1, p. 1, p. 352, n. 1.
[3] Eusebius, *De Vita Constantini* II, pp. 64-72.
[4] Cf. V. De Clercq, *Ossius of Cordoba* (Washington, D. C., 1954), pp. 221-228.

vokes the first great general council at Nicea in 325. So it is that out of the swirling currents of history and human affairs and divine aims which converge at Nicea there comes the unmistakable voice of authority to control minds and compel agreement. Guided by the Holy Spirit, the Council canonizes the term that will be the touchstone of orthodoxy and put an end to equivocation and ambivalence—*homoousios*—consubstantial. By this word the Fathers of Nicea state, for all the centuries, that Jesus Christ is truly the Son of the living God, equal to the Father in all things because he possesses the same numerically identical nature as the Father. Such is the interaction of the divine truth and the historical process which took place at Nicea. It is, for the Church of all the ages since, a lustrous and majestic moment which Christian generations have continued to admire and recall. Something of the Christian enthusiasm that surrounds this Council was captured by Eusebius of Caesarea when he wrote:

> When they were all assembled (at Nicea) it appeared evident that the proceeding was the work of God inasmuch as men who had been widely separated not only in sentiment but also personally by difference of country, place and nation were brought together and comprised within the walls of a single city forming as it were a vast garden of priests composed of the choicest flowers. . . . Constantine is the first prince of any age who bound together such a garland as this with the bond of peace and presented it to his Savior.[5]

II

As a second general point I would submit that the place of the general councils in the teaching of the Church might be very much illumined by seeing them in their relationship to the whole corpus of Catholic teaching. Viewed this way the general councils stand like a series of great mountain peaks, each one of which enables us to comprehend in one sweeping perspective the teaching effort that leads up to them and the doctrinal and theological development that flows down from them. Looking back from

---

[5] Eusebius, *op. cit.*, 3, 6-7 (trans. Richardson, The Nicene and Post-Nicene Fathers 1, 521).

these high historic points, one can see in an almost patterned vista the main roads as well as the by-roads along which popes and bishops and theologians gradually ascended each of these heights. Clearly seen too, as part of this process, are the difficulties and obstacles as well as the religious, social, and political forces that either impeded or demanded or set in motion the demand that brought about the convocation of the council. Standing on these same conciliar heights, we can also turn our eyes forward and see how each of these councils played a part in the future development of Catholic teaching by the impulses they gave to theologians and the orientations they communicated to succeeding theological efforts. Evident too is the fact that these councils have imparted direction and impetus to the spiritual and devotional life of the faithful, and out of this also has come a further penetration of God's revealed mysteries, which has played its part ultimately in the teaching of the Church. In fine, studied from this standpoint, as summing up the past and giving rise to the doctrinal currents that will shape the future, it is possible to plumb the full riches of conciliar teaching much more fruitfully. In the light of this perspective one can begin to see how dogmas are indeed a structure formed by the Holy Spirit and rising from the supernatural life that animates the Church and informs her divinely guided history.

While this thesis might be illustrated by any one of the general councils, none is so satisfactory an example as the one which seems to be the greatest, namely, Trent. This is true, first, because this Council sums up broad areas of past teaching and brings to bear on its issues the teaching of past councils as well as an extensive amount of biblical and patristic resource and joins to them an extraordinarily rich development of scholastic theology. Out of these doctrinal resources it produces a synthesis and explanation of Catholic teaching on a scale hitherto unknown. Second, its main dogmatic concern is with what is the very heart of the Christian life, that is, grace and the sacraments, whereby the individual, through God's gifts, is translated from the kingdom of darkness into the light and kingdom of the Son of God. Third, and particularly relevant here, is the fact that at this Council, through its actual activity and direction, is resolved an issue that had wracked and torn the teaching work of the Church for more than two centuries. This issue is the relation of the general council to the pope. It is this issue, jurisdictional on the surface but, in fact, involving the very constitution of the Church and the proper nature of a general council, that I should like to employ to substantiate my thesis.

For the modern Catholic who lives in the doctrinal climate produced by Trent, the Vatican Council, and the work of the modern popes, the situation on the eve of Trent is almost inconceivable. Hence if the work of Trent is to be made fully intelligible and properly appreciated, we must imaginatively stand on the height of Trent and try to see as a whole the two hundred years that precede that Council. Only by seeing in this historical vista something of the clash of aims and ideas and the turmoil of events shall we be able to evaluate the peculiar character of the issue of papal primacy as it presented itself to the Council. Only by seeing it as a whole shall we be able to understand why the Tridentine Fathers and particularly the papal legates resolved the issue the way they did. For it was this very issue of papal primacy that had made the effort to convoke a council a major struggle in itself, entailing a series of futile and unsuccessful efforts that had left even the genuine Catholic reformers almost in despair. Even when the Council did meet, there were large numbers of both Catholics and Protestants who were convinced that it would toll the knell of the papal claims to ecclesiastical supremacy.

Underlying and giving force to this apprehension of disaster was the fact that during the great Western Schism a whole corpus of revolutionary ideas about the Church and the papacy had come to the fore and taken deep root in the minds of men. These ideas are not produced by the Schism but the Schism makes them viable on a large scale. These ideas are summed up by Msgr. Philip Hughes thus:

[The] catastrophe [of the Great Western Schism] came at the end of a century when the whole strength of the politicians had been exerted to compel the Church to retire from all concern with temporal affairs;

in an age when thinkers would have had it retire from the field of thought, and mystics would divorce its piety from the pursuit of truth; the trader, too, will be pleased if religion will now abandon its claim to regulate the morality of exchanges, and Marsiglio's ideal is only slumbering that will satisfy all of these by making religion a matter of rites alone and of activities within a man's own soul.[6]

It is in this climate of ideas that the Great Western Schism occurs and becomes one of the worst calamities that have befallen the Church. The result is:

> Forty years of wandering in a wilderness where no one knew with certainty who was the head of the Church, a forty years in which unity of belief was indeed marvellously preserved but in which administrative chaos reigned and there sprang up an abundance of new anarchical theories about the nature of the papacy and its role.[7]

There must be, then, some consideration of these revolutionary ideas about the role of the papacy and the correlative conciliar theories. They take their rise with the coming of the new lay state under such men as Philip the Fair of France. Their object is to give legitimacy to the claim of absolute power by the prince. To do this they must destroy all papal claims to sovereignty, even spiritual. The most thoroughgoing exponent of this is Marsilius of Padua who is in fact the real theoretician of the lay state.[8] For Marsilius the Church is but the religious aspect of the state. Even as the state exists only because of the will of the majority to form such a group, so also the will of the majority of the faithful both brings the Church into existence and is the source of all its religious authority. In logic, therefore, Marsilius holds that the authority of general councils derives from this same source, as well as the right to depose and excommunicate. In such a group the Pope can be no more than the delegate and servant of the general council where the will of the majority is expressed.[9]

---

[6] *A History of the Church*, III (New York, 1947), 228-229.
[7] *Ibid.*
[8] Cf. G. DeLagarde, *La Naissance de l'esprit laique* (Paris, 1957). Vol. II treats of Marsilius under the subtitle "Marsile de Padoue ou le Premier Theoricien de l'Etat Laique."
[9] *Ibid.*, p. 190.

Similar to this theory but more carefully nuanced and more conscious of the complexity of the problem is the position of William of Ockam. The Franciscan thinker emphasizes the principle that all authority depends on representation and hence a council has authority only because it is representative of the whole Church. Likewise, since the Pope receives his authority from a human agency and there is nothing directly divine about his office, he can be deposed or other popes elected as representation requires them.[10]

Both these theories are totally alien to the canonical tradition of the West, and yet by the time of the second generation of the Schism, leading canonists like Francis Zabarella have begun to make them their own.[11] The reason is clear enough. It is a desperate situation and it is felt desperate measures are needed. The older canonical theory of John of Paris that would let the general council depose a Pope in the extraordinary case of heresy no longer suffices; a radical solution must be sought. In such a mental atmosphere the agent of the French king, Pierre d'Ailly, Bishop of Cambrai, uses these theories to advance the absolutism of the king and settle the schism by destroying the primacy of the Pope. He maintains that it is only a matter of pious belief that a general council is infallible but it is erroneous to hold that the Pope is infallible. The papacy and its authority are a purely practical matter intended only to secure good government. Hence a council may judge a Pope not only for heresy but for refusing to obey its conciliar authority.[12] Persuaded by such thinking, men now begin to agitate for a council based on these theories. Their agitation succeeds and a council is gathered at Pisa in 1409, but it does not end the schism; it worsens it by beginning a third line of popes. The important thing, though, is that Pisa gave public recognition and currency to these theories, even if for emergency reasons. Five years later these theories become full-fledged principles of action at the Council of Constance. For, whatever the juridical devices involved, the Council of Constance gathers under the authority

---

[10] E. F. Jacob, *Essays in the Conciliar Epoch* (London, 1943), p. 93.
[11] Cf. Hughes, *op. cit.*, p. 275.
[12] *Ibid.*

of the civil rulers and the solution, as they see it, is worked out in accord with these new principles. Hence while for the canonist the authority of the council might remain ambiguous, yet for the generality of the European world it appeared to consecrate as a principle the superiority of a council over the Pope.[13]

The consequences of the solution achieved at Constance create the situation with which Trent is ultimately faced. From 1417 on, the papacy can only fight a rear guard action against the encroachments of the civil rulers. No longer is the Pope the unquestioned cornerstone of Christendom, and so the ambiguity of the solution of Constance is exploited again and again by the Christian princes to serve their own ends both political and financial. The popes themselves feared a new general council which would enlarge on the theories that had ruled at Constance. Nor was this an idle threat, since for almost a quarter of a century Christendom was the witness of a legitimately convoked general council, meeting at Basel, which set itself up as the supreme authority in the Church and attempted to make its own the historical, papal prerogatives, both doctrinal and jurisdictional. Finally, from the very beginning of Lutheranism as a popular heresy until it becomes an organized church, every effort to confront the movement or to exercise effective doctrinal authority was paralyzed or rendered useless by the device of an appeal from the Pope to a general council. In the words of Msgr. Hubert Jedin:

> With this reservation "until the general council" numerous compromises had been agreed to (in Germany) which though many did not realize it replaced the Catholic way of life by another. A confusion of ideas such as Catholics of today are scarcely able to imagine made it possible for a generation reared in the Catholic faith to die out and for another to grow up fashioned by the teaching, the worship and the propaganda of Protestantism. The opening of the Council came only just in time to preserve the Latin nations from a similar calamity; for the northern ones it was too late.[14]

Such then is the tragic dilemma that stems from the Great Western Schism and the conciliar solution attempted at Con-

---

[13] Cf. Hefele-Leclercq, *op. cit.,* T. VII p. 1, p. 592.

[14] *A History of the Council of Trent* (New York, 1957), I, 580.

stance. A general council is desperately needed, but no Pope will hold one for fear that the principle consecrated at Constance will bring worse disasters for the Church and particularly for the papacy. Yet, basically, the princes refused to cooperate with a council that did not in some way maintain the principle of Constance. If, on the other hand, the Pope or a general council convoked by the Pope were to proclaim the primacy of the Pope over the council, all the decades-old wrath and propaganda which had been implanted in so many minds would render the council useless. It is this dilemma that haunted the popes all during the development of Luther's revolt. Either it made them procrastinate or inhibited them altogether from calling a council. Only a man who combined tact and determination joined to a vision of the overwhelming needs of the Church could face such an issue. Such a man was Paul III, who succeeded to the papal throne after the disastrous reign of Clement VII. The first of the reforming popes, Paul III, was an experienced diplomat, highly intelligent, tenacious and resolute. Above all he saw clearly that the only hope of restoring the prestige of the papacy and making its authority effective was through a policy based not on power politics but on the Church's own proper view of herself as the instrument of salvation. It took ten years, but the combination of these things finally brought about the convocation and formal opening of the Council of Trent in December of 1545. In the history of the Church it was a great moment which is recorded by Seripando, the General of the Augustinians, in his diary thus: "The door is now open, the mouth is open that only utters unadulterated truth; the tribunal is set up which alone can examine and decide all controversies; it is for this purpose that the Council has been demanded and convoked."[15]

However, if the Council were to utter unadulterated truth, it must be truly an ecumenical council, an organ of the teaching Church, not a kind of parliament or convention after the pattern of Constance and Basel. It was the achievement of Paul III and his successors who followed his lead that Trent did in fact become an organ of the teaching Church. The process by which this was

---

[15] *Concilium Tridentinum* (Freiburg, 1901 ff.), II, 409.

accomplished is simple enough in concept; the Pope without public statement or fanfare or political negotiation acted in accord with the ecumenical tradition that goes back to the early Church and exercises the papal prerogative recognized by antiquity, that he is the head of the Council. To implement this prerogative he makes full use of the College of Cardinals. Either in a meeting as a whole or by way of small individual commissions, every project of the Council is considered and discussed; suggestions are sent or, in some cases, a schema on the subject is proposed for the guidance of the Council as in the matter of justification. The Pope is most careful to leave the conciliar Fathers freedom of debate and allow them to change the suggestions and schemata as they saw fit. Frequently, however, the sterility of the debate and the inability to come to a decision obliged Pope Paul to intervene personally or through his legates and bring about a conclusion on which they could agree. During the sessions the Pope himself as well as his Secretary of State and the Apostolic Secretariat keep up a continual correspondence with the Council and the legates. Gradually, as the Council extends in duration, the Secretary of State becomes the interpreter of the mind of the Holy See and the instrument through which the Pope pursues his conciliar program.

At the scene of the Council itself this papal direction is made immediate through the legates. All the popes under whom the Council met selected their legates most carefully. Most of those chosen, like Contarini and Pole and Cervini and del Monte and Morone, were men who had come up through the curia as convinced proponents of reform and were dedicated to its achievement. By training and experience joined with learning and intelligence they had proved themselves capable of realizing this program. The popes sent four and even five legates to the sessions, forming a kind of commission with a president so that they might pool their experience and sustain one another in the critical moments. The legates themselves keep in constant communication with Rome so that their efforts are harmonized with those of the Pope. In addition, the legates are given a staff of eminent canonists to act as officers of the Council. As it eventuates, these men come to serve as the intermediaries between the Council and the Pope and so facilitate that collaboration of the two, which is of the essence of a true general council. All these things thus entered into the daily activity of the Council, and by means of them the papal direction and influence were interwoven into its very fabric. Out of this there comes into being a vital and continuous collaboration between the teaching Church and its Head; a collaboration which makes of the Council of Trent a true organ of the solemn magisterium through which the teaching Church indefectibly communicates God's revealed truth. It is true that the Council does not define this papal primacy, but by the time the Council ends no one doubts that the Pope had exercised a true and accepted supremacy over the Council. What this meant for the Church is summed up by Ranke, the Protestant historian of the papacy:

> The great and immeasurable success (of the Council) was to see the bishops solemnly pledge themselves to observe the decrees of the Council of Trent and to see them submit themselves to the Pope by a personal profession of faith they swore to follow. The first projects conceived on the occasion of the Council looked to limiting the Pope but far from being executed these projects were completely destroyed. His power emerges from the conflict more extensive and stronger than it had ever been. The Pope keeps the exclusive right to interpret all the canons of the Council of Trent; he remains the sole master who prescribes the rules of life and imposes the rule of faith. The whole direction of the restored discipline finds itself more than ever concentrated at Rome.[16]

In addition to this the Council makes it clear that the dream of the conciliarists of running the Church by means of biennial general councils was a mirage. The conciliar machinery was far too cumbersome, complex, and slow ever to be an ordinary instrument of ecclesiastical government. To those who were willing to see, it was clear that the ordinary and most efficacious instrument for Catholic unity was the exercise of the authority invested in St. Peter and his successors by Christ. Though appeals from the Pope to a council will still be made, they fade away bit

---

[16] L. Ranke, *Die Römische Päpste* (Leipzig, 1874 ff.), I, 345.

by bit because Trent has made it clear that these are essentially political or schismatic subterfuges having no foundation in Catholic doctrine nor legal basis in the Catholic canonical tradition. It is hardly surprising, therefore, that the next ecumenical council after Trent makes explicit what was implicit in the total activity of Trent, that by divine institution the Pope has a primacy of jurisdiction and is infallible when he speaks *ex cathedra*.[17]

So much, then, for the work that leads up to Trent. At this point let us look forward from Trent and see something of the consequences that flow from its doctrinal teaching. The first thing to be noted here is in the realm of theology itself. The dogmatic affirmations of Trent codified centuries of Catholic teaching, and with these defined, sureties became points of departure for new theological reflection. For example, in the light of the Tridentine definition of justification as a supernatural and intrinsic transformation of man there gradually appears a rich theological development of the doctrines of sanctifying grace and merit. Correlatively the dogma that affirms that the work of salvation is a collaboration of divine grace and human liberty brings about extensive studies and reflection on actual grace and the mystery of our predestination. Any study of these theological reflections and their systematization demonstrates that the century that follows Trent is one of the great ages in the life of Catholic theology. It suffices here simply to recount the names that illumine the post-Tridentine world: Bellarmine, Melchior Cano, Dominic and Peter Soto, Toletus, Suarez, Vasquez, De Lugo, Banez, John of St. Thomas. All these and many others testify to the enormous impulse given theology by the Council of Trent. Integrally a part of the contribution of the Council to the teaching office of the Church is the establishment of the seminary, one of the principal organs of the ordinary magisterium of the bishop. Without a doubt nothing has so effectively supplied a steady flow of trained and qualified pastors of souls. In fact, it might well be argued that the seminary has had the largest share in shaping the life of

---

[17] Denzinger-Bannwart, 1821-1839.

the Church as it has confronted the divided Christianity that is the mark of the modern world.

No account of the influence of Trent would be complete if it did not mention the influence of the Tridentine teaching on Catholic life itself. As Monsignor Michel has noted, the sessions on original sin, justification, and the sacraments constitute in themselves an admirable code of holiness.[18] To read and study the decree on the sacrament of penance is to be made aware of God's mercy and the Christian standards we must live by, yet be brought to realize that God will not save us without our cooperation. Even the precise theological phrasing of the decree on the Eucharist does not conceal the profound love of the Church for the Sacrament of the altar. The majestic loveliness of the decree on the Mass offers untold material for contemplation, both theological and affective. All this is surely abiding proof of that inexhaustible fecundity which, as Vatican Council I teaches, is a mark of the divine character of the Church.[19]

III

As a final illustration of the place of the general council in the teaching of the Church, I should like to make explicit what has been implicit in all that has been said up to this point. It is that in the normal course of events it has been the ecumenical councils that have formally recognized and affirmed the fact of a dogmatic development having taken place. It is through the councils that we see much of this development; as a matter of fact, not only the history but the very existence of the general councils is proof that, as Cardinal Newman so perceptively pointed out, dogmatic development is inherent in the very nature of revelation and its transmission by an infallible teaching Church. For revelation is a fact that is transmitted as an idea. Because it is a living idea in the minds of men, it will be subject to that growth in understanding that is an exigency of all human intelligence. Subtly but

---

[18] Hefele-Leclercq, *op. cit.*, T. X, p. 1, p. xi.
[19] Denzinger-Bannwart, 1794.

steadily the consequences and bearings of this idea and its relationship to other truths, both human and revealed, will be developed. The challenge of controversy and the catalytic effect of error and disagreement will play their part. The faith and devotion and piety of the faithful under the impulse of the Holy Spirit will furnish additional insights into the meaning of the revealed truth. Dogmas already proclaimed and their theological elaboration will help to explicitate what is implicit. Exegetes and theologians will bring to bear the analogy of Catholic faith and doctrine, and so under this light penetrate further into the implications of this doctrine. Then, under God, at a given point in this historical yet divinely guided process, an ecumenical council will gather, and protected by the Holy Spirit as an indefectible and infallible organ of the teaching Church, it will consider and weigh this whole elaboration, and, if it judges fit, proclaim that this is a true development of dogma.

Instances of this are as manifold as the councils themselves. We might adduce that development at once Trinitarian and Christological encompassing Arianism, Apollinarianism, Nestorianism, and Eutychianism out of which after more than two hundred years comes the definition at the Council of Chalcedon that in Christ there are two distinct natures, each complete in itself, the one divine and the other human, and they are substantially united in the Person of the Word.[20]

Of equal interest, in the light of the coming ecumenical council, would be a study of the development of the dogma on the procession of the Holy Spirit from the Father and the Son. This would involve a consideration of the differences in doctrinal expression between the Greek and Latin Fathers as well as the discussions of these differences at the Council of Florence when the Greeks admitted that there was no doctrinal divergence.[21] To be incorporated into such a study would be the situation that caused the local Council of Toledo to formulate this expressly in the seventh century.[22] Especially relevant would be the intro-

---

[20] Denzinger-Bannwart, 148.
[21] Cf. J. Gill, *The Council of Florence* (New York, 1959), pp. 181-228.
[22] Denzinger-Bannwart, 277.

duction of the *"Filioque"* into the Creed, first in Gaul and then throughout the West. Germane to this whole study would be the struggle between Rome and Constantinople over Photius in which the *"Filioque"* becomes a permanent symbol of the conflict.[23] Finally we come to the second Ecumenical Council of Lyons, a re-union council, where the dogmatic development is solemnly affirmed and accepted in the words: "The Holy Spirit proceeds eternally from the Father and the Son as from one principle and . . . from a single spiration."[24] There are many others that could be used to exemplify this role of the ecumenical council, but by way of conclusion I should like to take an instance which is peculiarly relevant to modern times, and that is the relationship of faith and reason.

The problem of faith and reason is posed the moment that Christianity becomes an important factor in the life of the Greco-Roman world. For this Hellenic culture, like our own Western culture, is the heir of Greek thought and therefore has as its core an outlook that is essentially rational. Christianity, on the other hand, is a revealed religion and so communicates a body of truths whose acceptance and certitude rest, not on rational demonstration, but on faith and authority.

Moreover, many of the revealed truths of the Christian religion are supernatural mysteries that can be neither refuted nor verified by reason. In such confrontation there will necessarily be tension as well as conflict. If conflict arises, it will be from one or the other of two sources. There will be those who would make reason autonomous and reject all that cannot be subjected to its norms. This is rationalism in the pejorative sense. The other source of conflict, however, is a problem to be found in the very household of Christianity itself. It arises from the fact that the revealed truths are intellectual propositions and therefore capable of being objects of rational inquiry. Yet to inquire, to seek to understand, necessitates the introduction of rational considerations and concepts into the study of revelation. What then are the areas of

---

[23] M. Jugie, *Le Schisme Byzantin* (Paris, 1941), p. 143 et seq.
[24] Denzinger-Bannwart, 460.

revelation open to such inquiry? What are the norms that are to guide such a search? What is the line of demarcation between faith and reason? The answers to these questions, as the history of Christian thought shows, range all the way from a complete fideism to a total subordination of revelation to the norms and exigencies of natural reason.[25] It is a permanent problem of Christianity, differing from age to age only in the intensity with which it enters the intellectual life of the time. Yet until the 19th century there is only one brief dogmatic statement on faith and none at all on the relationship between faith and reason.[26]

In the 19th century, however, the Church through the instrumentality of the Vatican Council does formulate a dogmatic codification of its traditional teaching on the nature of faith and the relationship of faith and reason. Behind this codification lies not only the work of Augustine and Thomas Aquinas and the 16th and 17th century theologians but the fact that this issue has taken on an enormously destructive dimension. In the name of reason and science the heirs of the Enlightenment had mocked and scorned and rejected the very idea of a supernatural order and revelation. The world they sought to create had neither need nor place for faith or grace or the Church. Far more deadly, however, and far more permanent was the Kantian experiment that limited all certain knowledge to knowledge acquired through the physical sciences. Transcendent principles in general and religious truths in particular could have no objective basis in the philosophy of Kant and his heirs. Faith in religious truths could only be a pragmatic thing.[27]

Living in the world created by such ideas, Catholics began to diverge along one of two ways. Some, either because they despaired of reason or because they were disgusted by the bloody results of the French Enlightenment, completely rejected individual reason as a source of certitude. In the place of individual reason

---

[25] Cf. E. Gilson, *Reason and Revelation in the Middle Ages* (New York, 1948), pp. 3-66.
[26] Cf. Denzinger-Bannwart, 798.
[27] Cf. E. Gilson, *The Unity of Philosophical Experience,* (New York, 1937), pp. 223-247.

they set up what comes to be called "Traditionalism," a system of thought that makes of social authority and, supremely, the Pope the sole source of all moral and religious truth. In this group we find men such as de Bonald, de Maistre, Lammennais,[28] Bautain,[29] and Bonnetty.[30] In Germany, on the other hand, a number of Catholic thinkers, seeking to produce a theology acceptable to the university world, accept as a basic premise some form or other of the Kantian experiment. Making this their point of departure, they attempt to establish the certitude of Catholic dogmas on a scientific basis. The failure of this effort is evidenced by the condemnations of Hermes and Günther and Frohschammer.[31] In the midst of this intellectual crisis a number of theologians begin the study of St. Thomas, whose own achievement is the fruit of a like grave crisis over the relationship between faith and reason.[32] This study produces a widespread revival of scholasticism as well as theologians of the caliber of Franzelin and Kleutgen who play leading roles in the preparation for the Vatican Council and its actual deliberations.

Such then is the immediate background to the teaching of the Vatican Council on faith and reason. It is worth noting in this regard too that the importance of this teaching has been frequently by-passed or overshadowed by the more highly publicized controversy over the opportuneness of the definition of papal infallibility. Yet the fact is that the issue of faith and reason is the first order of business at the Council, and by far the greater amount of the time the Council was in session was spent on this matter.

In the actual conciliar discussion the Fathers are guided by the preparatory work of the theological consultors and very much dependent on their advice during the Council. Every point is discussed in detail in the Council itself, and there is full freedom of discussion. The final draft of each point is arrived at only after

---

[28] Cf. Denzinger-Bannwart, 1617.
[29] Cf. Denzinger-Bannwart, 1622.
[30] Cf. Denzinger-Bannwart, 1649 et seq.
[31] Denzinger-Bannwart, 1618 et seq.; 1655 et seq.; 1666 et seq.
[32] Cf. C. Dawson, *Medieval Essays* (New York, 1959), pp. 129-137.

extensive discussion and careful re-writing that takes into account all suggestions and criticisms. To anyone who has studied carefully the history of the problem of faith and reason in the Church, the skill with which the Fathers of the Council single out the fundamental elements of the Catholic tradition is itself a strong indication of the guidance of the Holy Spirit. How effectively they carried out their teaching office is eloquently witnessed to by a careful reading of the Vatican decree *Dei Filius*,[33] which both culminates and canonizes a development reaching back to the earliest years of the Church. Thus in precise and measured phrase they define the unique nature of infused faith:

> This faith however which is the beginning of human salvation the Catholic Church asserts to be a supernatural virtue by which, with the aid and inspiration of God's grace, we believe that what He has revealed is true—and this not because its intrinsic truth is perceived by the natural light of reason but because of the authority of God who reveals it and who can neither deceive nor be deceived.[34]

The Council unequivocally affirms the absolutely supernatural character of the revealed mysteries:

> For the divine mysteries so transcend the created intellect that even when they have been given in divine revelation and received by faith they continue to remain veiled by faith itself and wrapped in a kind of mist as long as in this mortal life we are exiled from the Lord.[35]

Solemnly professed is the unbroken Catholic tradition that faith and reason are two distinct orders of knowledge:

> The perpetual universal consent of the Catholic Church has held and now holds that there is a twofold order of knowledge distinct not only in origin but in object. They are distinct in origin because in one we know by means of natural reason and in the other by means of divine faith. They are distinct in object because, in addition to what

---

[33] Denzinger-Bannwart, 1781-1820.

[34] *Ibid.*, 1789.

[35] *Ibid.*, 1796.

natural reason can attain to, there are proposed for our belief mysteries hidden in God that cannot be known unless divinely revealed.[36]

Yet while these two orders are clearly distinct, the Council confirms the long held doctrinal tradition that they are in harmony:

Although faith is above reason there can never be any real disagreement between them since the God Who reveals mysteries and infuses faith is the same God Who endows the human soul with the light of reason, and God cannot deny Himself any more than truth can contradict truth.[37]

Then the Council proclaims that not only are faith and reason in harmony but, as Catholic theology proves, they can mutually assist one another:

Not only are faith and reason unable to disagree but they are mutually advantageous inasmuch as right reason demonstrates the foundations of faith and, illumined by the light of faith, cultivates the science of divine things; faith on the other hand frees and safeguards reason from errors and supplies it with a manifold knowledge.[38]

It might be most fitting to end this treatment of the teaching of the Vatican Council with its statement that is the *raison d'etre* of a School of Theology such as this:

It is nevertheless true that if human reason illumined by faith carries on its inquiries in an earnest and devout and prudent way it can, with God's help, attain to some understanding of the divine mysteries and that a most fruitful understanding not only from the analogy of the things that it knows naturally but also from the connection of the mysteries amongst themselves and with the last end of man.[39]

Viewed against the whole history of Catholic theology these statements of the Vatican Council solemnly testify that the Church through its solemn magisterium has determined that a true dog-

---

[36] *Ibid.*, 1795.
[37] *Ibid.*, 1797.
[38] *Ibid.*, 1799.
[39] *Ibid.*, 1796.

matic development has taken place and irrevocably professed that this development is an integral part of the deposit of faith. And though it has clothed its thought in theological language and given to it a sense of elevated and dispassionate calm, still its work seems worthy of the lovely tribute Cardinal Newman paid to another conciliar effort:

> Cautiously lowering the truth, wrapping it in reverent language and so depositing it in its due resting place which is the Christian heart.[40]

Eugene M. Burke, C.S.P.

---

[40] J. H. Newman, *Arians of the Fourth Century* (New York, 1908), p. 137.

The General Council
in the History of the Church

The General Council
in the History of the Church

THESE CHAPTERS are concerned primarily with the theological discussions and teachings of the ecumenical councils. There is room, however, for a treatment which, without neglecting the theological side of the general councils, will attempt to place them in their historical settings, to sketch the political and physical conditions under which they assembled and held their sessions, and thus to view them not only in the light of church history alone but also in that of universal history as well.

The council as a device for dealing with matters of ecclesiastical doctrine and discipline has an Apostolic origin, for it was inaugurated by the meeting of the Apostles and presbyters held in Jerusalem in the year 49. A dispute had arisen at Antioch between certain Judaeo-Christians and Paul and Barnabas regarding the necessity of circumcision for salvation, and the question was referred to the Apostles and presbyters in Jerusalem. After a long and heated debate, in which Peter took a leading role and was supported by James, it was decided that Gentile converts to the new faith should not be required to submit to the rite of circumcision as prescribed by the Law of Moses. At the same time it was proposed "to send written instructions to the Gentile converts to abstain from anything that has been contaminated by idols and from immorality and from anything strangled and from blood." Representatives were then sent to Antioch along with Paul and Barnabas bearing a letter containing the decree and moral instructions of the meeting held at Jerusalem.

This meeting at Jerusalem is of the highest significance in the history of the Church. It was called and conducted by the Apostles themselves under the acknowledged leadership of Peter. A doctrinal question and certain moral problems were freely and even heatedly discussed for a long time before a decision was reached. When the decision was once made, it was accepted by all; and the doctrinal decision and moral instructions of the Council were then officially promulgated by letter to the Christian community at Antioch. The Council of Jerusalem in its composition, in its leadership, in its decisions and their promulgation, exemplified the solemn teaching authority of the Church and set a pattern for the future.

Our sources tell us nothing more about ecclesiastical councils before the second half of the second century. Their frequency and rapid development from that time can only be adequately understood against the background of the rapid spread of Christianity and the need of an increasingly more elaborate ecclesiastical organization and administration to preserve unity of faith and purity of morals in the midst of a hostile pagan intellectual and social environment, and under a pagan state whose head demanded worship as a god and which had outlawed the new religion and persecuted it, if not always and everywhere with the same rigor and intensity.

Christianity was first established in the cities throughout the provinces of the Roman Empire, and usually first in the provincial capitals. Since the other cities of a given province were ordinarily Christianized by missionaries from its capital, it was only natural that the provincial capital should be regarded as the mother-city of the other Christian communities in the province, and that its bishop should enjoy special prestige and authority. It was only natural, too, under the circumstances, that the boundaries of ecclesiastical provinces should be made to coincide with those of the civil administration. From the early fourth century the special honor and authority of the bishops of provincial capitals was formally signified by the title of metropolitan which was henceforth given to them. The Bishop of Rome, as the successor of St. Peter, enjoyed a unique primacy throughout the

Church. It would be wrong, however, to think that his juridical primacy was fully developed and universally recognized in a post-Tridentine or post-Vatican sense. The bishops of the venerable sees of Antioch and Alexandria had much greater prestige and authority than other metropolitans, and thus the foundations were being laid before the close of the third century for the later patriarchates. Finally, for various reasons, the bishops of Ephesus, Caesarea of Cappadocia, Caesarea of Palestine, and Carthage claimed and were accorded special privileges not enjoyed by the majority of metropolitans.[1]

As the Church increased in numbers and the Christian community exhibited an ever wider geographical distribution, the problem of communication in the interests of preserving unity of faith, of dealing effectively with moral disorders, and of maintaining the primitive spirit of fraternal Christian love became steadily more difficult. In New Testament times and in the age of the Apostolic Fathers, the personal visit and the letter addressed to the community rather than to a specific individual served as bonds of union. But as the life of the Christian communities became more complex, something more was needed, especially to deal with heretical teachings and questions of discipline. Hence, as noted above, we find frequent mention, from the second half of the second century, of provincial meetings or councils as an effective device for discussing questions of faith and morals and for formulating decisions and regulations in common.[2]

According to Apollinaris of Hierapolis, quoted by Eusebius, synods held in Asia examined the tenets and practices of the Montanists, condemned them, and expelled the Montanists from the Church. Eusebius quotes also a passage from a letter of Serapion of Antioch which refers to a synod held in Thrace deal-

---

[1] On the development of ecclesiastical organization down to the Peace of the Church, see the pertinent chapters by J. Zeiller in Fliche-Martin, *Histoire de l'Eglise depuis les origines jusqu'à nos jours* 2 (Paris, 1935), 394-421; and Bihlmeyer-Tüchle, *Kirchengeschichte* 1 (12th ed.; Paderborn, 1951), 110-117 (with copious bibliography).

[2] On the rise of local and provincial councils, see the references given in n. 1. For a detailed treatment, see Hefele-Leclercq, *Histoire des conciles* 1.1 (Paris, 1907), 125-212.

ing with the same problem and taking the same action. The Pascal Controversy occasioned the convening of numerous synods in East and West in the early third century, of which it will suffice to mention in particular those held at Caesarea of Palestine under Theophilus and Narcissus of Jerusalem, and at Rome under Pope Victor.

In 251 Pope Cornelius summoned a council of sixty bishops at Rome which condemned the rigorism of Novatian in dealing with the *lapsi.* It thus confirmed the similar action taken by a council held under St. Cyprian at Carthage a short time before. Three new councils were convened at Carthage between 254 and 256 which dealt especially with the question of the validity of baptism conferred by heretics or schismatics. The persistence of St. Cyprian and the other African bishops in denying the validity of baptism so conferred involved them in a bitter controversy with Pope Stephen, the successor of Cornelius, who declared that baptism so received was valid. Cyprian found an ardent supporter for his own position in Firmilian, bishop of Caesarea in distant Cappadocia. Pope Stephen died in 257 and was succeeded by Pope Sixtus II, a friend of St. Cyprian. The point at issue was not settled, but friendship was restored between the sees of Rome and Carthage. In the heat of controversy, the great Cyprian, who died a martyr's death in 258, raised the question of the relation between the Pope and the episcopate which was not destined to be definitively answered before 1870.[3]

The heretical Christological teachings of the brilliant but unscrupulous Paul of Samosata, bishop of Antioch, occasioned the convening of three councils in that city between 263 and 268 before he was eventually condemned and expelled. Among the bishops who attended these councils were Firmilian of Caesarea of Cappadocia, Gregory and Athenodorus of Pontus, Helenus of Tarsus, Hymenaeus of Jerusalem, Theotecnus of Caesarea of Palestine, and Maximus of Bostra. Dionysius, bishop of Alexandria, was invited but was too feeble to make the long journey. One partisan of Paul of Samosata must be especially mentioned:

---

[3] On the councils called by St. Cyprian and on his relations with Rome, see J. Lebreton, "Saint Cyprian", in Fliche-Martin, *op. cit.,* 2.186-210.

the priest Lucian of Antioch, teacher of Eusebius of Nicomedia, Maris of Chalcedon, and Arius of Alexandria. In many respects he is to be regarded as the true father of Arianism.[4]

The Council of Elvira, held in Spain c.304, was attended by nineteen bishops from all parts of the Spanish peninsula, among them Ossius of Cordoba, who was to play such a major role in the history of the Church during the next fifty years. Twenty-six priests sat with the bishops, but the bishops alone subscribed the canons of the council. The eighty-one canons are all disciplinary and deal with a wide range of topics: baptism, marriage, clerical celibacy, consecrated virgins, idolatry, use of images, relations of Christians with pagans, Jews, and heretics; vigils, cemeteries, usury, etc.[5]

The council held at Rome in 313 and that held at Arles the following year have a special importance. They were the first councils or synods that met following the Peace of the Church, and the first in which the Roman Emperor played a role of any kind.[6]

In the interests of peace in Africa, Constantine recognized Caecilian as the lawful bishop of Carthage. Donatus and his adherents charged that Caecilian's ordination had been invalid, and they petitioned the Emperor that judges be selected from the bishops of Gaul to examine and decide the case. Constantine then ordered that a meeting should be called at Rome under Pope Miltiades on October 1, 313, at which the Pope, with three bishops from Gaul and a fourth named Mark selected by the Emperor, should hear the arguments of ten African bishops from each of the opposing parties and pass judgment. Pope Miltiades summoned in addition fifteen bishops from all parts of Italy and the meeting was thus transformed into a council. This council met in the Palace of the Lateran—first mentioned in this connec-

---

[4] On the councils of Antioch which condemned Paul of Samosata, see J. Lebreton, "L'Eglise d'Antioche à la fin du IIIe siècle", in Fliche-Martin, *op. cit.*, 2.345-352.

[5] On the Council of Elvira, see Hefele-Leclercq, *op. cit.*, 1.1.212-264, and V. C. De Clercq, *Ossius of Cordoba: A Contribution to the History of the Constantinian Period* (Washington, 1954), 85-117.

[6] On the Councils of Rome and Arles, see J. R. Palanque, "L'affaire donatiste," in Fliche-Martin, *op. cit.*, 3 (Paris, 1936), 41-52, and Hefele-Leclercq, *op. cit.*, 1.1.272-298.

tion in ecclesiastical history—on October 2-4, 313. The council, after hearing both sides, decided unanimously that Caecilian was the lawful bishop of Carthage. Donatus himself was the only member of his party formally condemned.

The Donatists were not satisfied and again appealed to the Emperor. After a judicial investigation, he found that the Donatist charges against Felix of Aptonga, the consecrator of Caecilian, were false. He then invited by letter all the bishops of the West to meet in a council at Arles in August, 314, to deal with the Donatists, and he ordered that the *cursus publicus* should be available for their use. Forty-six sees were represented at the council, with bishops, priests, or deacons coming from Gaul, Italy, Dalmatia, Spain, Africa, and Britain. Pope Sylvester was represented by two priests and two deacons. The synodal letter sent to the Pope informs us that the Donatists were condemned and expelled. The Donatists again appealed to the Emperor in person and Constantine reopened the case, which he handled in a vacillating and confusing fashion for two years. Finally, he lost his patience and dealt with the Donatists independently, and with a ruthlessness that was in striking contrast to his preceding handling of the question.

By the beginning of the fourth century, the local, provincial, or regional council, though always handicapped by the fact that Christianity was under the ban of the State, even when it was not being actively persecuted, had become an indispensable instrument of the Church for dealing with questions of doctrine and discipline and for promoting unity of faith. With the establishment of the Peace of the Church, a new era begins in the history of the councils. The Council of Rome held in 313 and that of Arles held in the following year even received active support from the Emperor, but it was a support combined with his direction. Imperial participation in ecclesiastical affairs was first invited by the Donatists, but given the structure and traditions of the Roman State and the imperial office, it was inevitable that it would take place. It is against this background that one must interpret the conduct of the zealous Ossius of Cordoba as well as that of the ambitious court bishop, Eusebius of Nicomedia.

In their joy at deliverance from nearly three centuries of persecution, Christian bishops could hardly be expected to perceive that Constantine's handling of the Donatist affair was ominous for the future. He reopened the Donatist question after two councils, convoked in succession by his orders, had unanimously decided in favor of Caecilian and condemned the Donatists. He thus seriously impaired the authority of the two councils, which had acted properly and decisively within their own sphere, and then, after further bungling, lost patience with the Donatists and dealt with them more savagely than the situation demanded.

The Church, without yet realizing it, was embarking on a long and formidable struggle with Christian emperors who inherited the lofty absolutism of their office from pagan predecessors who had enjoyed divine status. Posing as defenders of the Faith—which in practice will be the faith to which they subscribe—they will tend to regard themselves as superior to all bishops, and even to the Pope, in matters ecclesiastical, and they will try to make the Church a department of the State. Caesaro-Papism has its beginnings under Constantine. St. Ambrose, Pope Gelasius I, and Gregory the Great will in turn see the danger threatening the Church at the hands of the imperial power, and each will define the proper relations of Church and State in clear and uncompromising language. But their pronouncements will often be ignored or repudiated in the long history of the Church.

The Council of Arles in 314, in spite of the large number of bishops who attended it and their wide distribution, and in spite of the presence of papal representatives, was not a general or ecumenical council. Without question, however, it set the pattern for the first of the ecumenical councils, that of Nicea, convoked ten years later. Donatism had led to the calling of the Council of Arles. It was only natural that the much greater problem of Arius and his teachings should occasion the calling of a similar body to deal with it.

The Christological heresy of Arius of Alexandria will be dealt with in detail in another chapter. Let it suffice to observe that Arius, as noted earlier, was a disciple of Paul of Samosata and that his theological speculation was yet another attempt of a man trained in the Greek philosophical tradition to reduce a sublime truth of faith, the mystery of the Trinity, to the measure of human knowledge and experience. He was thus led to deny the eternity and divine nature of both Christ and the Holy Ghost, and their equality as divine Persons with God the Father in the Trinity. On being condemned by an Egyptian synod convoked by his bishop, Alexander of Alexandria, in 320 or 321, Arius took refuge in Caesarea in Palestine and subsequently in Nicomedia, the imperial capital. He was welcomed there by his old school friend Eusebius, who was now bishop of that city. Eusebius was powerful because he enjoyed the special favor of Constantia, the sister of Constantine and wife of the Emperor Licinius. Within a very short time, the whole Christian East was divided into two opposite groups: the bishops of Egypt and their adherents under the leadership of Alexander of Alexandria condemning Arius, and the bishops of Asia and their adherents under Eusebius of Nicomedia supporting him.

Constantine, after his defeat of Licinius, came to Nicomedia in 324 and received Eusebius' version of the controversy. Not being satisfied, and alarmed at the serious disruption of internal peace in the empire, he ordered his trusted ecclesiastical advisor, Bishop Ossius of Cordoba, to go to Alexandria. The idea of calling the Council of Nicea probably came out of the meeting of Ossius and Alexander, although it is possible that the Synod of Antioch, which met to elect a successor to Bishop Philogonius at the beginning of 325, may have proposed that such a council be convoked at Ancyra. At any rate, Constantine, whether at the suggestion of Ossius and Alexander or on his own initiative, decided that a council should be convoked at Nicea in 325, selecting that city because of its accessibility to the bishops of the West as well as to those from the East—and also because it was so close to Nicomedia, his capital at this time. As in the case of the Council of Arles, the facilities of the *cursus publicus* were placed at the disposal of the bishops invited to come to Nicea.[7]

---

[7] On the Council of Nicea, see G. Bardy, "Les origines de l'Arianisme et le Concile de Nicée," in Fliche-Martin, *op. cit.,* 3.69-95; Hefele-Leclercq, *op. cit.,* 1.1.386-632. On the role of Ossius of Cordoba at the Council, see especially V. C. De Clercq, *op. cit.,* 197-289.

Between 200 and 300 bishops answered the imperial summons and attended the council. The actual number is not known. The traditional figure of 318 is first found in St. Hilary's *Contra Constantium* 27 (360 A.D.) and is obviously reminiscent of the 318 servants of Abraham mentioned in Gen., 14:14. The great majority of the bishops at the Council were from Egypt, Palestine, Syria, and Asia Minor, but there was a good representation from Greece and the adjacent Greek-speaking regions. From the Latin-speaking provinces only the following are known as having come to Nicea: two bishops from Moesia and Dacia, Mark of Calabria, Caecilian of Carthage, Nicasius of Gaul, and Ossius of Cordoba in Spain. Pope Sylvester could not attend, owing to age, but he sent two Roman priests as his representatives. A few bishops were also present from the Caucasus, Greater Armenia, and Persia.

A number of the bishops were outstanding theologians, among them Eustathius of Antioch, Alexander of Alexandria, Eusebius of Nicomedia, and Marcellus of Ancyra. Alexander was accompanied by his deacon, Athanasius, a young man of twenty-five, who was to exhibit in the theological discussions of the Council the religious zeal, moral courage, and intellectual brilliance which distinguished him through a long career and made him the greatest champion of Catholicism against Arianism. Mention should be made, too, of the participation of the great church historian, Eusebius of Caesarea, of the saintly Spiridion of Cyprus, and of men like Paphnutius the Egyptian, Paul of Neo-Caesarea, and Amphion of Epiphania, whose blinded eyes or broken bodies bore moving testimony to their sufferings for the Faith in the persecution of Diocletian. Despite the few Westerners present, it is significant that Ossius of Cordoba, the most trusted of the ecclesiastical advisors of Constantine at this time, served as president of the Council.

The first meeting of the bishops was held on May 20, 325, in the main hall of the imperial palace at Nicea. Constantine entered, wearing the full regalia of his office, and delivered an address in Latin which was immediately read to the assembly in Greek translation. The Emperor, contrary to legend, did not interfere in the deliberations of the bishops during the Council. Arius was given full opportunity to state his teaching before he was condemned. There was long and sharply divided discussion, however, before the fathers were able to draw up a symbol which should express accurately and unambiguously the traditional doctrine on the divinity of the Son of God. The word *homoousios* in the meaning of *consubstantial* was finally adopted. The Easterners did not like the word too well because it had been used in an heretical sense by Paul of Samosata and Sabellius, that is, to signify that the Father and the Son are identical in person. Rome, on the other hand, had long favored the use of *homoousios* in the sense of *consubstantialis,* and it would seem that Ossius of Cordoba pushed strongly for its acceptance, All but two bishops signed the Symbol of Nicea, although Eusebius of Nicomedia, among others, did so very reluctantly. The Council then dealt with the Meletian Schism, settled the Easter Question, and formulated a comprehensive series of canons which were to apply to the universal Church.

The great assembly closed on June 19, a month after its convocation. As this date coincided with the twentieth anniversary of Constantine's accession to power, he invited the Fathers of the Council to attend an elaborate banquet prepared as a part of the celebration. The spirit of peace and cordiality which marked the close of the Council was more apparent than real, for the bishops who sympathized with Arius and his teaching were already planning to reject *homoousios* and to renew their efforts in his favor.

The Council of Nicea marks an epoch in the history of the Church. Local, provincial, and regional councils had become recognized and practically necessary instruments for dealing with dogmatic and moral questions—in particular, with those that were the object of wide and serious dispute or controversy—and for preserving unity of faith and promoting Christian morality. The dogmatic decisions and disciplinary canons, however, of councils even as important as those of Carthage, Antioch, Elvira, and Arles, unless subsequently confirmed by the head of the Church, the Bishop of Rome, and thus given a greater prestige and a wider application, were confined in their effect to their respective provinces or regions, apart from their voluntary adoption in other areas. The Council of Nicea, however, was convoked as a universal council to deal primarily with the question of Arius. It was universal in its membership, as it was actually attended by representatives from all parts of the Christian world, and its dogmatic decisions and disciplinary canons were regarded from the first as being authoritative and binding throughout the whole Church.

The Council of Nicea and the seven ecumenical councils that followed it differ from all later general councils in two respects. In the first place, they were convoked by Roman and Byzantine emperors, and they were all held in the East. Western representation, however important it might be in authority, was always small. Because of its special nature, as will be noted below, there was no Western representation at all at the Second Ecumenical Council, that of Constantinople in 381. In the second place, it was customary for the Emperor as well as the Pope to give formal approval to the dogmatic definitions and disciplinary canons of these councils. The papal approval, furthermore, did not always assume the formal and solemn character which we have come to associate with ecumenical councils and which we emphasize in our definition of the ecumenical council, especially since the Council of Trent. It should be noted, too, that the Council of Constantinople of 381 was convoked by the Emperor Theodosius the Great as an assembly of Eastern bishops only. It is only from the sixth century that it was recognized as an ecumenical council and ranked in authority with Nicea and Chalcedon.

Yet the first eight councils must be regarded as truly ecumenical, for they fulfill the spirit, if not the strict letter, of our canonical definition. There is no uncertainty about their ecumenical character or authority in ecclesiastical history and tradition. Gregory the Great, for example, compares the first four general councils to the four Gospels, because they defined the basic dogmas of the Church, namely, her teachings on the Trinity and on Christ. Father H. Jedin, the distinguished historian of the Council of Trent, has handled the problem of the convocation of the early councils very well. The following paragraph is worth quoting:

The question whether the early councils were convened by the emperors with the previous consent of the Bishop of Rome, or even by his commission, has been the subject of controversy from the time of the Reformation. . . . As far as the facts go, the question may be answered in the negative, but the basic rights of the Popes are in no wise affected. It is equally certain that, as Patriarchs of the West and by virtue of a unique pre-eminence, they were represented; that their legates always received a special place of honor and occasionally presided over the sessions; and that papal approval of the conciliar decisions was an indispensable condition for their universal validity.[8]

The Western Church recognizes twenty councils as ecumenical, but the acceptance of certain councils as ecumenical was a matter of dispute as late as the Council of Trent. Cardinal Robert Bellarmine (1542-1621), who had made special investigations in the history of the councils, was the first to introduce the enumeration of the ecumenical councils that has come to be regarded as traditional.[9]

The twenty ecumenical councils span nearly sixteen centuries in the history of the Church. They thus reflect the conditions and problems of widely different periods in the life of the Church and in the world in which she carries out her divine mission. It will be useful to group the ecumenical councils as Father Jedin has done, and to characterize them from the general historical point of view.

The first six ecumenical councils—First Nicea (325), First Constantinople (381), Ephesus (431), Chalcedon (451), Second Constantinople (553), and Third Constantinople (680-681)— were primarily concerned with defending and defining the teaching of the Church on the Trinity and on Christ, the Second Person of the Trinity. The Seventh Ecumenical Council, or Second Nicea

---

[8] See H. Jedin, *Kleine Konziliengeschichte. Die zwanzig oekumenischen Konzilien im Rahmen der Kirchengeschichte* (Freiburg im Br., 1959), 15. See also the English translation by E. Graf, O.S.B., *Ecumenical Councils of the Catholic Church: An Historical Outline* (New York, 1960), 14. Unfortunately the English translation has been carelessly edited and has to be used with care. For convenience, the English translation will be cited in these notes, but with my own modifications or corrections. Jedin's little book is a timely and excellent historical outline of the general councils. For details, Hefele-Leclercq, *Histoire des Conciles*, is still the basic work, but it has to be supplemented on many points by later studies.

[9] See Jedin, *op. cit.*, 3-5; Hefele-Leclercq, *op. cit.*, 1.1.79-91.

(787), was convoked to settle the question of the veneration of images. The Eighth Ecumenical Council, or Fourth Constantinople (869-870), dealt with the Photian Schism. As a result of the scholarly investigations of the last thirty years, we have a much better understanding of this last Council and of the issues involved, and we have been led to regard Photius in a much more favorable light. The Catholic Church numbers this Council of 869-870 as ecumenical. The Greek Church does not, but regards as the Eighth Ecumenical Council the synod convoked by Photius in 879-880.[10]

During the period of the first six councils, the Pope, despite his unique position of authority in the religious sphere, was in his civil capacity a subject of the Emperor. This explains why emperors, who in keeping with an inherited imperial tradition regarded themselves, in practice if not in theory, as supreme in ecclesiastical as well as in civil affairs, did not hesitate to employ even physical violence against the Pope in their effort to secure papal approval for their own religious beliefs and policies.

In the eighth century, however, a radical change took shape in respect to the civil status of the Pope. Owing to the rise of Islam and to internal weaknesses in the Byzantine Empire, the Pope of necessity became the *de facto* ruler of Rome and the vicinity. When threatened by Lombard encroachment, and with no help coming from the Byzantine Emperor, Pope Stephen III (752-757) appealed to Pepin the Frank whose royal consecration he had recently confirmed. Pepin took up arms against Aistulf, king of the Lombards. After intermittent war and peace, he defeated him decisively and placed Rome and the regions reconquered from the Lombards, including Ravenna, under the authority of the See of St. Peter. The Pope was thus made a temporal ruler in his own right, independent both of the Lombards and the Byzantine Empire. It is significant that Pope Hadrian I (772-795), less than a generation later, ceased to date his official acts by the regnal years of the Byzantine Emperors and was the first Pope to issue

---

[10] On the Photian Schism, see especially E. Amann, "L'affaire de Photius," in Fliche-Martin, *op. cit.*, 6 (Paris, 1937), 465-501; F. Dvornik, *The Photian Schism: History and Legend* (Cambridge [Mass.], 1948).

his own coinage. But sovereignty in the temporal order and, above all, the extent of the territory in which temporal rule had to be exercised were destined to impose burdens and problems on the papacy that could not have been foreseen by Pope Stephen III and his contemporaries. Msgr. Hughes has put it very well:

> The history of the next twenty years showed how seriously the complication of the Papacy's new political importance could distract the popes from the task of their spiritual rulership. . . . The problem that drove the popes to ally themselves with the Franks had by no means been solved. It had merely changed its form and in one form or another continued to worry the popes through the next twelve hundred years, to 1870 and to 1929, a problem they can never neglect, and preoccupation with which, not infrequently, must distract their energy from more directly spiritual affairs.[11]

The Eighth Ecumenical Council, Fourth Constantinople (869-870), closes, as we have seen, the list of ecumenical councils held in the East. All the rest of the General Councils, to use the term employed to designate them in the Middle Ages, have been held in the West. The general councils of the Middle Ages and the Renaissance fall into two main groups: the first, comprising the ninth to the fifteenth inclusive, and the second, the sixteenth, seventeenth, and eighteenth. The two general councils of modern times, the Councils of Trent and the Vatican, are best treated on an individual basis.

The general councils of the West had their beginnings in the synods convened by reform popes either at Rome or elsewhere. As the idea took legal form, under the influence of the Pseudo-Isidorian Decretals but not entirely so, that no synod embracing more than one ecclesiastical province could be called without papal consent, the papal synods themselves, under the leadership of able and zealous reform popes, gradually extended the range of their membership and took up questions of major concern to the universal Church. Among such synods, it will suffice to mention those at Pavia and Rheims convoked in 1049 by Pope St. Leo

---

[11] P. Hughes, *A History of the Church: An Introductory Study* 2 (New York, 1935), 165-166.

IX (1049-1054), the synod convened by the same Pope at Rome in 1050, the Roman synod held by Pope Nicholas II (1059-1061) in 1059, and especially the synods called by Pope St. Gregory VII in the course of his pontificate (1073-1085), and those convoked by Pope Urban II (1088-1099) at Piacenza and Clermont in 1095. It is through his synods that Gregory VII launched his comprehensive reform program, and it is before his synods likewise that Urban II made his eloquent appeal to Western Christians to take up arms and free their Eastern brethren and the Holy Places from the bondage of Islam. Gregory VII was the first pope, furthermore, to invite abbots as well as bishops to his synods and to encourage princes to send representatives with the privilege of participating in the discussions of certain questions of immediate and direct concern to them.

These papal synods helped the Church very much to establish her freedom and to assert her rights in the long and formidable struggle over investitures. At the same time, the active participation of numerous and influential bishops in their discussions and decisions gave the episcopate a new sense of its powers and importance. Accordingly, already during this period, we note the beginnings of the Conciliar Movement. Peter Crassus, for example, an adherent of the Emperor Henry IV (1056-1106), challenged the right of the Pope to convene general councils and maintained that this right belonged to the Emperor. The anonymous author of the *De unitate ecclesiae* declared that this unity was based, not on the authority of the Pope over the universal Church, but on the unity of the episcopate, bolstering his argument with a reference to St. Cyprian.[12]

In the light of the development of papal synods with such wide representation in their membership and of the powerful support which they furnished the Pope in the Investiture Struggle, it was natural enough that Pope Callistus II (1119-1124), the second successor to Paschal II (1099-1118), should desire to have the Concordat of Worms, which he had made with the German King Henry V in 1122, solemnly ratified by a synod or council. This,

---

[12] See Jedin, *op. cit.*, 63-64.

along with the need of legislation in the field of discipline, was
the occasion for his convocation of the First Lateran Council—
the Ninth Ecumenical and the first to be held in the West—in the
spring of 1123. As Hughes has observed: "In its preoccupation
with the practical problems of church discipline, the extirpation of
abuses, and its concern for the general social well-being, the council only reflected the close relation of the two societies, civil and
religious, and it set the pattern for all the other six councils of
the Middle Ages."[13] Its twenty-first canon made Holy Orders a
diriment impediment to marriage and thus laid down in definitive
fashion the law of clerical celibacy.

Only sixteen years later, in 1139, Pope Innocent II (1130-1143)
called the Second Lateran Council—the Tenth Ecumenical—to
settle the schism of Anacletus, to implement and carry further the
reform program inaugurated by Gregory VII, and to condemn
the errors of Arnold of Brescia and other heretical teachings.
Pope Alexander III (1159-1181) convoked the Third Lateran
Council—the Eleventh Ecumenical—in 1179. It decreed that
henceforth a two-thirds majority of the cardinals should be required in papal elections, it condemned the Albigenses, and it
drew up twenty-five additional *capitula* covering a wide range of
matters within the civil as well as the ecclesiastical sphere. The
Waldenses, contrary to a persistent erroneous statement still
found in many books, were not condemned at this Council, but a
few years later under Pope Lucius III (1181-1185) at the Synod
of Verona held in 1184.

The first three Lateran Councils were subsequently given ecumenical status on the basis of their large membership, importance
of questions discussed and decisions made, and the intention of
the popes who convened them. The Fourth Lateran Council—the
Twelfth Ecumenical—was, however, formally planned and convoked as an ecumenical council by Pope Innocent III (1198-1215)
on November 11, 1215. All bishops, except three or four exempted in each province, the heads of the Cistercians, Premonstra-
tensians, Hospitallers and Templars, abbots, temporal princes
and other civil rulers of all kinds, delegates from exempted

---

[13] Hughes, *op. cit.*, 2, 302.

bishops and from cathedral or collegiate churches, were invited. At the opening session there were present 412 bishops, 800 abbots and priors, representatives of the Emperor Frederick II and the Latin Emperor of Constantinople, of the kings of England, France, Hungary, Jerusalem, Cyprus, and Aragon, and even of many Lombard communes. The bishops of the Patriarchate of Constantinople had been invited but did not come—which is not strange in the light of the events of 1204. Owing to the tensions between the Pope and the Emperor Frederick II, the number of German bishops present was small. On the other hand, bishops came for the first time from Bohemia, Hungary, Poland, Lithuania, and Esthonia.

The acts of the Council are lost, but, as it held only three sessions in rapid sequence (November 11, 20, and 30), it is evident that an enormous amount of preliminary work had been done in the two years between the date of invitation (April 4, 1213) and the convocation. The Pope was apparently ready to present to the first session seventy elaborate *capitula* or decrees already formulated. The council issued a special symbol or profession of faith directed against the Albigenses, condemned the Trinitarian errors of Joachim of Flora, dealt with the question of a new crusade, and other matters. But its main work was in the field of reform. The decrees cover in realistic and practical fashion all ecclesiastical ranks and obligations, and every state and condition of society, and in considerable detail. Chapter 21, for example, lays down the law that every Catholic must confess at least once a year and receive the Holy Eucharist during the Easter time.

The Pope was a strong personality, but he did not dominate the Council to the extent claimed by J. Haller and others. The co-operative spirit with which the reform legislation was received and subsequently carried out, however imperfectly, would seem to refute such a charge. Furthermore, if the Council had supported the Pope's recommendation that the papal chancery and court be maintained by financial contributions from the whole Church, it is possible that the subsequent system of papal taxation and imposts which developed in the fourteenth century, and which caused such resentment throughout Europe, would not have arisen or become necessary. In respect to the relations of Church and State, Innocent III invaded the sphere of the State more than was necessary or prudent, but it is easier to see this in historical perspective than was possible in the early thirteenth century.[14]

The First Council of Lyons—the Thirteenth Ecumenical—was convoked at Lyons in 1245 by Pope Innocent IV (1243-1254), who had fled Italy to escape being made a virtual prisoner by the Emperor Frederick II. Lyons was chosen because of its central position, but also because it was a free city and could receive, if necessary, the protection of King Louis IX of France. The Council was called primarily to depose Frederick II, who had repeatedly broken his promises to respect the rights of the Church and was clearly bent on subordinating the Church to the State. He had done all in his power to prevent bishops from attending the Council, but some 140 were able to be present. Thaddeus of Suessa, the champion of Frederick, was given a full hearing, but after a thorough review of the Emperor's career, the Council at the session of July 17 deposed the Emperor from his office as German King and Roman Emperor. The Council also formulated a series of twenty-two *capitula* dealing with various ecclesiastical matters and urged a crusade against Islam—Jerusalem had been captured by the Saracens in 1244—and the Mongols. Innocent IV, one of the ablest and most courageous of the popes, has been severely criticized for his deposition of Frederick II, but he must be judged against the background of his age and the circumstances of the deposition. Frederick II, in spite of his brilliance and in spite of the sympathy that the tragic end of the Hohenstaufen dynasty naturally inspires, was an unscrupulous and ruthless individualist who persisted to the last in his attempt to deprive the Pope and the Church of powers and rights that properly belonged to the ecclesiastical sphere.

The Second Council of Lyons—the Fourteenth Ecumenical— was convoked by Pope Gregory X (1271-1276) on May 7, 1274. In his letter of invitation sent out in 1273, he had announced that the Council would consider the reform of papal elections, a new

[14] For a good exposition and evaluation of the Fourth Lateran Council, see Hughes, *op. cit.*, 2, 420-431, and especially 421-422.

crusade, and reunion with the Greeks. It was a truly international gathering in which all ecclesiastical and lay ranks were well represented. The Greek Emperor Michael did not attend, but he was represented by Germanus, Archbishop of Nicea, and by his chancellor. St. Thomas Aquinas had been invited, but died at Fossanuova near Rome on March 7, 1274, as he was on his way from Naples to Lyons. St. Bonaventure was present at the Council and, as a cardinal bishop, sat on the right of the Pope.

The Greek representatives signed the prescribed profession of faith; and in the singing of the *Credo* in Greek and Latin in the Mass that followed, they accepted the addition of the *Filioque* clause. Thereupon they were permitted to keep the traditional text of their own Creed. This union with the Greeks soon collapsed because Michael had proposed it for purely political reasons and it did not have the support of the Greek hierarchy. The reform decree on papal elections, *Ubi periculum,* with minor changes and additions, is still in force. Plans were finally approved for a new crusade some years hence, but such a crusade was now too late. Acre fell to the Mohammedans in 1291. The Dominican General, Humbert of Romans, among others, at the suggestion of the Pope had prepared recommendations on the reform of various abuses, and such documents undoubtedly played a part in the formulation of the thirty-one *capitula* issued by the Council. They deal, among other matters, with ecclesiastical elections and with the privileges of the recently founded Mendicant Orders—Dominicans, Franciscans, Hermits of St. Augustine, and Carmelites—and with their relations with the secular clergy. The Second Council of Lyons accomplished much for the Church, but the chief credit for its success must be given to Pope Gregory X, who showed such ability in planning and such determination, accompanied by tact, in carrying out what had been planned.

The Council of Vienne—the Fifteenth Ecumenical—was held in 1311-1312 by Pope Clement V (1305-1314), the first of the Avignon popes. Throughout his pontificate he was subjected to the pressures and threats of the powerful and unscrupulous Philip the Fair, who wished to make the papacy serve his own policies. Philip was especially bent on destroying the Templars and amassed all kinds of false testimony against them. The list of prelates invited to the Council was previously checked on the basis of a conference with Philip. The members of the Council included twenty cardinals, four patriarchs, twenty-nine archbishops, seventy-nine bishops, and thirty-eight abbots. Frenchmen and Italians constituted the largest number, but there were also present archbishops from Spain, England, Ireland, and Germany. The Council opened in the liturgical manner that will be employed later at Constance, Basle, and Trent. The presence of the Pope gave special solemnity to the occasion. The Pope then announced that the Council was to consider the question of the Order of the Templars, the reform of morals and freedom of the Church, and the recovery of the Holy Land. The examination of the charges made against the Templars and the ultimate condemnation of the Order are a long and tragic story.[15] A number of reform decrees covering clerical abuses were passed, but, in the unfavorable circumstances of the period, they were not really effective. The recovery of the Holy Land by force of arms gave way to the idea of a missionary crusade. On the recommendation of Raymond Lull, the Council ordered that chairs of Greek, Hebrew, and Arabic be established in universities to give training in the languages required for missionary work among Jews and Mohammedans, but little could be done to implement this decree because of the lack of qualified teachers.

The Council of Vienne was the last of the papal general councils of the Middle Ages. In all these councils, as Jedin well puts it, "the popes had given final form to the conciliar decrees and embodied a large number of them in the papal code of laws. At the councils the popes appear as the head of the Church and of all Christendom. . . . All this was changed when the councils came to be regarded as the 'representation' of Christendom and of all members of the Church, for whom constitutional rights were claimed."[16]

The Conciliar Movement is dealt with elsewhere in this volume. Let it suffice here to observe that the weakness of the papacy and

---

[15] See Hughes, *op. cit.*, 3 (1947), 99.
[16] *Op. cit.*, 103-104.

its loss of effective juridical authority and of moral prestige during the Avignon exile, and in the period of confused ecclesiastical affairs occasioned by the Great Schism, gave an impetus to the Conciliar Movement that it could never have had under normal conditions.[17] Two councils held in this period, namely, the Council of Constance (1414-1418), and that of Basle-Ferrara-Florence (1431-1449) are reckoned as the Sixteenth and Seventeenth Ecumenical Councils, but with definite limitations. Only the last sessions of the Council of Constance (XLII-XLV) and the earlier sessions approved by Pope Martin V (1417-1431) have an ecumenical character. The Council of Basle is not to be considered ecumenical beyond its twenty-fifth session. Furthermore, Pope Eugene IV (1431-1447) approved only a limited number of its decrees.

The Fifth Lateran Council—the Eighteenth Ecumenical—was convoked under Pope Julius II (1503-1513) in 1512 and was continued into 1517 by his successor, Pope Leo X (1513-1521). It marked a return to the pattern of the earlier Lateran Councils, but it was only a pale reflection of its predecessors. The Council was attended by fifteen cardinals and seventy-nine bishops, almost all from Italy. After declaring that the Council of Pisa (1511) was invalid, the members of the synod devoted their major attention to the question of a thoroughgoing reform of the Church. The general of the Augustinians, Aegidius of Viterbo, made an eloquent plea for reform, and later the two Camaldolese, Giustiniani and Quirini, presented Pope Leo X a long memorandum describing abuses with concrete suggestions for reform. Some reform decrees were approved, but Julius II and Leo X were papal princes of the Renaissance, not reform popes. The comprehensive and drastic reform of the Church, which was so badly needed, and which Luther's attack now made imperative, was destined to be the task of the greatest of the reform councils, that of Trent, which would be convoked under one of the ablest of the successors of St. Peter, Pope Paul III, in 1545.

---

[17] On the Conciliar Movement, see the excellent section in Jedin, *op. cit.*, 105-108, and the outstanding monograph of B. Tierney, *Foundations of the Conciliar Theory. The Contribution of the Medieval Canonists from Gratian to the Great Schism* (Cambridge [Mass.], 1955).

The Councils of Trent and the Vatican, the Nineteenth and Twentieth in the ecumenical list, are treated elsewhere in this volume. By way of conclusion, I should like to outline very briefly the difficulties of communication and of maintaining communication throughout the Church before the middle of the last century. The coming of the railroad, the steamship, and the telegraph began that marvelous development of the various forms of communication with which we have become so familiar in our own generation and the wonders of which were so strikingly brought home to us in the 1960 national election. The Vatican Council was the first general council in which its members had available modern means of transportation in the form of the railroad and steamship and the rapid communication made possible by the telegraph. It may be noted, too, that the first trans-Atlantic cable had only been laid three years before that Council met. The invention of printing (c.1450) practically coincided with the close of the Council of Basle (1449), but printed materials could not be disseminated rapidly before the rise of modern means of transportation. The press, which plays such an enormous roll in conveying information and in molding public opinion, likewise owes its phenomenal development to the modern means of transport and mechanical communication.

The conditions of travel and other means of communication during the whole period spanned by the ecumenical councils, including the Council of Trent, are also of interest. All travel was on foot, on horseback, by carriage, or by boats propelled by oars or sails. Under the Roman Empire, a splendid road system had been built up and was maintained by the government. Travel along the Roman roads was not rapid except in the case of the *cursus publicus,* but it was safe, and even large rivers were spanned by excellent bridges. The Christian emperors, as we have already noted, placed the *cursus publicus* at the disopsal of bishops who were attending councils sponsored by them. Sea voyages were always regarded as more dangerous than land travel and normally were not taken during the autumn and winter months. Hazards to health were constantly facing those taking long journeys—the physical weariness of slow and tiresome travel, constant changes in foods and water, and a complete absence of preventive medicines against fevers and other diseases to which travellers were exposed.[18]

Apart from personal contact through travel, communications in Church and State had to be maintained through letter or personal messenger. In the fourth and fifth centuries bishops employed priests and especially deacons as carriers of important communications in East and West, as they could be entrusted with verbal as well as written messages. All letters and all documents were written by hand, and every letter or document had to be reproduced by hand when additional copies were needed. Paper and parchment were likewise prepared as writing materials by a long and slow hand-process. Letters often travelled slowly, except when it was possible for bishops to make use of the *cursus publicus,* and they were often never delivered.[19] Forgery of letters and documents was fairly easy to perpetrate but hard to detect. It was often very difficult to repair the damage caused by the forgery, as is evidenced, for example, in the Arian controversies of the fourth century.[20] The most famous of mediaeval forgeries, the Isidorian Decretals, were accepted as genuine during the whole second half of the Middle Ages, and even much later, and played a very important role in conciliar history and in papal policy in general. The recognition of their true character and the establishment of Le Mans or its vicinity as their place of composition c. 850 is one of the triumphs of modern historical criticism at its best.[21]

Communication in the Middle Ages and in Modern Times before the middle of the nineteenth century was, in general, slower

---

[18] For a detailed treatment of travel by public and private means of transportation in the fourth and fifth centuries A.D., see D. Gorce, *Les voyages, l'hospitalité, et le port des lettres dans le monde chrétien des IV⁰ et V⁰ siècles* (Paris, 1925), 3-133. See also L. Friedländer, *Roman Life and Manners under the Early Empire.* English trans. by L. A. Magnus. 1 (London, n.d.), 268-299.

[19] M. R. P. McGuire, "Letters and Letter Carriers in Christian Antiquity," *The Classical World* 53 (1959-1960), 148-153, 184-185, 199-200; D. Gorce, *op. cit.,* 193-247.

[20] See G. Bardy, "Faux et fraudes littéraires dans l'antiquité chrétienne," *Revue d'Histoire Ecclésiastique* 32 (1936), 5-23 and 275-302.

[21] On the Pseudo-Isidorian Decretals, see Amann, "Les faux isidoriens," in Fliche-Martin, *Histoire de l'Eglise* 6 (Paris, 1937), 352-366.

than under the Roman Empire, was much more difficult, and was far less safe. It is enough to recall in this connection the conditions of communication to the 1830's within our own country and with Europe and other parts of the world. But in addition to the physical difficulties and dangers of travel and the enormous personal expense that it involved, bishops in the Middle Ages and in Modern Times down to the Council of Trent—and even later—were often forbidden by emperors and kings to leave their realms to attend even papal councils. This happened especially, of course, when the papacy was in conflict with rulers like the Emperor Frederick II and Philip the Fair. But even Charles the Fifth did not hesitate to put obstacles in the way of convoking the Council of Trent until he decided that the general political situation was favorable to his own interests.

Finally, a word should be written on the all-important subject of language. The majority of the Western bishops in the age of Constantine were still bilingual, but extremely few Easterners had any appreciable knowledge of Latin. In the second half of the fourth century, and especially in the fifth and sixth centuries, the decline of Greek in the West was very rapid. Pope Leo the Great had to rely on Latin translations of the acts and decrees of the Council of Chalcedon. Pope Gregory the Great (590-604) tells us that he did not know Greek himself and that it was practically impossible to find a competent translator of Greek in Italy, and that at Constantinople no one could be found capable of translating Latin into Greek.[22] This breakdown in linguistic communication between East and West was a major factor in the misunderstandings that so often arose on doctrinal questions, and the resulting cultural cleavage was an underlying cause of the Greek Schism.

Latin as the universal official language of the Church in the West has played an historical role that can hardly be exaggerated in preserving unity of doctrine and culture. It is being called upon again to perform its function as the basic official language of communication in the coming ecumenical council, which will be the

[22] M. R. P. McGuire, "The Decline of the Knowledge of Greek in the West from c. 150 A.D. to the Death of Cassiodorus," *Classical Folia* 13., No. 1 (1960), 3-25.

largest and most truly universal of all such meetings that have been held in the long history of the Church.

Modern technology has made it possible for bishops to come from the remotest corners of the earth to Rome in less time than it took their sixteenth-century predecessors to travel from Florence, or even from Naples, to the Holy City. It has likewise made possible an unbelievably rapid dissemination of news on the work of the new council to all parts of the world. It will even enable men everywhere to hear announcements made by the living voices of the Pope and his representatives. The longing for closer communication between bishops widely separated from each other in the ancient *oecoumene,* the world of the Greeks and Romans, a longing repeatedly described in moving words in their letters, is now being fulfilled in our generation in a manner that was beyond the range of the most vivid imagination of earlier times.

Martin R. P. McGuire

Christ the God-Man: The Councils
of Nicea and Ephesus

Christ the God-Man: The Councils of Nicea and Ephesus

THIS CHAPTER will concern itself with the specific work of two councils—Nicea and Ephesus—and the role they played in the definition and explicit formulation of the doctrine that lies at the very basis of Christianity, the fundamental truth of all Christianity, the doctrine that our Lord Jesus Christ is both true God and true man.[1]

"Who do men say the Son of Man is?" the Master asked his disciples one day near Caesarea Philippi.[2] They answered that some said John the Baptist, others Elias, others Jeremias or one of the prophets. The Master persisted, "But who do you say that I am?" And Simon Peter answered, "Thou are the Christ, the Son of the living God." This is the answer of faith, the answer of divine revelation. It is the answer the Church details and renders safe from human misunderstanding in the solemn words of the Credo of the Mass: "I believe in one Lord, Jesus Christ, the only-begotten Son of God, born of the Father before all ages; God of God, Light of Light, true God of true God; begotten, not made, of one substance with the Father, through whom all things were created. For us men and for our salvation, He came down from Heaven, and by the Holy Spirit was made flesh of the Virgin Mary, and became man."

---

[1] Editor's note: Father Benard had not completed the preparation of this paper before his tragic death. It was thought better, however, to publish it substantially as it was found among his effects.

[2] Matt. 16:13-16.

53

This serene, clear, and unambiguous expression of the Faith of the Church concerning our Lord was not arrived at in a moment, or without effort. In its present form it is the work of centuries of patient operation of the Church's teaching office, protected by the charism of infallibility and under the providential doctrinal guidance of the Holy Spirit. It is, however, substantially the work of Nicea, and one of its most important aspects was gloriously proclaimed and stoutly defended at Ephesus. To examine, even in summary fashion, the role of these two great councils is to be rewarded with additional insight into the manner in which the Spirit of Truth guides the Church through all the vicissitudes and ambiguities of history and in the end makes all things work for good.

Nicea and Ephesus are at once awe-inspiring divine dramas and fantastic human ones. Great figures move across the ancient stage: Athanasius and Cyril of Alexandria, Ossius of Cordoba, Eusebius of Nicomedia and Eusebius of Caesarea, Popes Sylvester I and Celestine I, the Emperors Constantine and Theodosius II, the heresiarchs Arius and Nestorius. Proud cities are involved, and their ambitions: Antioch, Alexandria, Constantinople. Famous schools of theology, Antioch and Alexandria, oppose to one another their different approaches to the Sacred Scriptures. With a combination of subtlety and violence, men dispute the meaning of crucial words—*ousia, homoousios, hypostasis, prosopon, theotokos*. Men are intransigent, men are conciliatory, men are hasty, men are vacillating, men are kind, and men are cruel. And all these elements we have mentioned are only samples, not a catalogue, of the myraid strands in the tapestry whose colors perhaps are human, but whose plan and outline are divine.

Quite obviously, no single chapter can possibly take into account all—or even a considerable part—of the personages or the doctrinal details involved in the controversies of Nicea and Ephesus. Moreover, records are fragmentary; some accounts are far from impartial; about many details distinguished historians still disagree. But the main and crucial lines of the story are clear enough, and are all that we can possibly address ourselves to in this chapter.

I. *The Council of Nicea*

Nicea today is a quiet little town, barely noticed by the guide-books, rarely visited by tourists. Its small cluster of dwellings hugs the shore of its handsome lake, far within the circuit of the powerful walls that even in ruins convey to us some idea of what an important city it once was. There is a partially excavated arena that seems to have held about ten thousand people, and some considerable remains of the basilica of St. Sophia that in 787 housed the Second Council of Nicea—not the one with which we are concerned. Nicea is now called Iznik and is in the northwest corner of Asia Minor (present-day Turkey) about sixty miles from Constantinople, or, as it is now named, Istanbul. To this city, easily accessible, with an even, spring climate, graced with one of his provincial palaces, Constantine the Great summoned the bishops of the Christian world to council in the year 325.

The part played by the Emperor in the summoning of the Council, as well as many of the physical details of its conduct, have been clearly explained in other chapters of this volume. Let us concern ourselves with the doctrinal issues involved. The Council was called to deal with the teachings of Arius. Who was Arius, and what did he teach?

Arius was a native of Libya, born about the year 256. He received his theological training at Antioch, where great stress was laid on the literal meaning of the bible text together with the historical and grammatical study of its sense. Such an approach, of course, is a legitimate and necessary one, but it seems quite clear that the spirit of Antioch tended to rationalism and to the elimination of the element of mystery from Christian teaching. Ordained fairly late in life, Arius was appointed to the suburban church of Baucális at Alexandria. He was well past middle age when his particular and peculiar teachings about the Son of God came to the attention of the Bishop of Alexandria, Alexander.

It is not easy, incidentally, to gain a clear idea of the personality or the general appearance of Arius. He was, to say the least, a highly controversial person, and about such persons, descriptions are likely to differ. Epiphanius calls him "downcast in visage, with manners like a wily serpent." Alexander speaks of his melancholy temperament. A modern historian writes:

> There was nothing insignificant about him, neither his intelligence, character, violence, nor ambition. His handsome, emaciated face, his air of modest austerity, the serene but vibrant severity of his speech— all seemed made for seduction. In consequence he drew around him crowds of fanatical young women. He was a scholar certainly, with a natural flair for dialectic that only an oriental permeated by the Hellenic spirit could possess. Everyone considered him a virtuous man, one who used himself harshly, devoted to penitential and ascetic practices, surrounded by an aura of dignity, almost of sanctity.

What was the teaching with which Arius attracted large crowds? He began with the idea of the absolute and ineffable grandeur and perfection of the Godhead—a noble and valid position. But from that position he proceeded to reason that such grandeur and infinite perfection could not be communicated, and that therefore outside of God everything is created and finite, including Christ, the Word of God. The Word, the Son of God, was a creature; a perfect creature, yes; the first begotten of all creatures, yes; but still a creature. Arius himself, in a letter to Eusebius of Nicomedia, exposes his position clearly. "We are persecuted," he wrote, "because we say that the Son had a beginning, but that God was without beginning. This is really the cause of our persecution; and likewise, because we say that He is from nothing. And this we say because He is neither part of God, nor of any subjacent matter."[3] There was indeed to be, in the whole course of the Arian heresy, much arguing from Scriptural texts, much discussion of the Ante-Nicene writers, much expression on the part of the Arians of their agreement with certain orthodox expressions for which evasions had already been found; but Newman put it clearly in his *The Arians of the Fourth Century* when he commented:

> The plain question was, whether our Lord was God in as full a sense as the Father, though not to be viewed as separable from Him; or whether, as the sole alternative, He was a creature; that is, whether

---

[3] Cf. John Henry Cardinal Newman, *The Arians of the Fourth Century* (London: Longmans, Green and Company, 1890), p. 213.

He was literally of, and in, the one Indivisible Essence which we adore as God, 'consubstantial with God,' or of a substance which had a beginning. The Arians said He was a creature, the Catholics that He was very God; and all the subtleties of the most fertile ingenuity could not alter, and could but hide, this fundamental difference.[4]

It was indeed a fundamental difference. In fact, no heresy so fundamental has been preached in two thousand years of the history of the Church. If the Son be not God, there is no Incarnation, no Redemption; "the whole of Christianity crumbles away and is emptied of its substance."

The saintly and learned Bishop Alexander first entreated and then commanded Arius, who by now had many followers, to desist from such preaching. Arius refused. Alexander summoned the Egyptian hierarchy to a synod at Alexandria. Nearly one hundred responded. Arius was condemned and deprived of his post. But he was by no means defeated. He gained the support of his former fellow student at Antioch, now the powerful and influential court bishop, Eusebius of Nicomedia. The controversy raged. Finally the Emperor, concerned for the political peace of his realm, summoned to Nicea the bishops of the world. They met, between two hundred and three hundred of them, at the imperial palace on May 20, 325. Alexander's judgment against Arius was solemnly confirmed.

So much for the bare historical facts. Let us return to the doctrinal matters which are our special concern here. The Fathers of the Council, indeed, condemning Arius were faced with the problem of formulating in clear and unmistakable fashion the true relationship of Father and Son. This they did in several phrases of the Creed of Nicea,[5] professing that the Son was "from the substance of the Father," that He is "true God of true God," that He is "begotten, not made." But it is in the famous and fateful expression *homooúsion to patrí* (of one substance with the Father, *consubstantial* with the Father) that they summed up and concentrated the full force of their reply, by asserting the full and perfect and co-equal divinity of the Son.

---

[4] *Ibid.*, pp. 253-254.
[5] DBEnch. 54.

For the theologian, the use made by the Fathers at Nicea of the word *homoousios* is surely the most technically interesting feature of the Council. It is the earliest expression of the full and complete control the teaching authority of the Church has and must have not only over the words it chooses in its formulae, but also over judgment as to the meaning of those words.

Homoousios is, of course, a compound word, made up of *homós* (one and the same) and *ousía* (substance, essence). The older and still more probable opinion is that it was proposed by Ossius of Cordoba, theological advisor of Constantine and presiding bishop of Nicea. But the fact is that, looked at only in itself, *homoousios* was a word not only ambiguous but suspect, especially to the prelates of the East. *Ousía,* as J. N. Kelly rightly observed,[6] had many meanings, according to its context and the philosophical allegiance of the user. At the Synod of Antioch in 268, Paul of Samosata had actually seen the word condemned when he had used it as meaning that the Son was the same *Person* as the Father. At the other end of the scale of meaning, Aristotle himself had used the word to denote, not identity of substance one and the same, but rather a general similarity of nature, as when he spoke of the stars as being consubstantial with each other. The Neoplatonists used the word in this latter sense also. We know that many of the orthodox, non-Arian bishops were not comfortable with the word; that they would have preferred a term taken from Sacred Scripture to safeguard the true Faith. But the Arians were subtle disputants from Sacred Scripture, and were interpreting the Scriptural expressions in their own way. The Fathers of Nicea, then, defended the true *meaning* of the word of Scripture by a term taken from outside of Scripture—a word, moreover, whose philosophical ambiguity they transcended, and whose meaning in *this* context—the context of divine truth—they authoritatively declared.

I do not wish to imply, of course, that the sense attached to *homoousios* by Nicea was an illegitimate sense; the sense attached was fully justified; but other senses could be used and had been

---

[6] Cf. John Norman Kelly, *Early Christian Doctrines* (New York: Harpers, 1958).

used; what Nicea professed was "this is the sense *here.*" May I stress again that the Church is a teaching *authority;* and that authority was demonstrated at Nicea in Bithynia in the year 325.

And so Nicea defended, with the human terms at her disposal, the clear tradition that the Son was truly God. But the controversy resumed practically as soon as the Council was over. Two of the bishops had refused to subscribe to the profession of faith to begin with; three others, including Eusebius of Nicomedia, soon withdrew their signatures. The Emperor supported now one side, now another. The subtleties of Semiarianism tortured men's minds and hearts. Athanasius, who at the Council had been an eloquent young deacon accompanying the Bishop of Alexandria, himself succeeded a few years after to the See of Alexandria and began his long career of struggle and exile for the truth. Arius banished, then recalled, was seemingly on the point of being restored to full communion in Constantinople on the demands and threats of Constantine when he (Arius) died suddenly in 336. Arianism actually fell to pieces when it seemed close to victory. At Constantinople in the year 381, at the Second General Council, the Creed of Nicea was secured.

II. *The Council of Ephesus*

About fifty miles by road southeast of Smyrna (or Izmir, as it is now called) on the Aegean seacoast of modern-day Turkey, there is a dusty little town called Selcuk. There is a Moslem-Byzantine citadel frowning over the town from the heights, and below the town a narrow valley of fig orchards and marshes runs eastward to the sea. In this valley, against the dark mass of Mount Coressus to the south, can be seen the gleam of marble ruins, the ruins of Ephesus, once one of the greatest of Graeco-Roman cities, and a city which is, for the Christian, one of the holiest spots on earth.

This is a city St. Paul knew well. Here lived St. John, and probably for a time our Lady also. It is tempting to speak of the memories of those we find there, and to discuss, for instance, the

arguments pro and con for the burial place of John and the house
that is by local tradition associated with our Lady. But let us go
at once to the center of the ancient town, near the once busy and
thriving harbor now silted over into a marshy plain. Here stand
the ruins of the Church of St. Mary, probably the earliest and
oldest of the great basilicas that have been raised in her honor.
The Church of St. Mary in Ephesus must not be thought of as
some small country church. It is a tremendous triple church, with
a huge entry hall and two long naves built one behind the other
and connected through the curved rear wall of the forward church.
The roof of the church is gone now, of course, and the upper part
of the walls; but the ruins still rise in places about twenty feet
above the ground, some of the creamy marble is still in position,
and the beautiful baptistery is still almost intact.

On June 22, 431, here in this church, 159 bishops and a deacon
representing the absent Bishop of Carthage met to consider and
judge the teachings of Nestorius. Who was Nestorius, and what
did he teach?

We must first note that the theological perspective of the
Nestorian controversy is not the same as that of Arianism.
Arianism, as we have seen, was concerned with the relationship
of the Word, or Son of God, to the Father. The faith defined was
that the Son is of the same substance as the Father, like the Father
eternal, like the Father uncreated, with the Father coequal. The
great controversy of the first part of the fifth century, on the other
hand, is concerned, not like Arianism with the full divinity of the
Son, but with the relationship of the divine and human natures in
Christ. That the divine nature is fully and coequally divine is not
questioned. But how is the divine nature united to the human
nature?

But to return to Nestorius. He was born sometime after 381
in Syria, of Persian parents. Like Arius, he studied theology at
Antioch, and became a famous preacher of that patriarchal see.
In 428 he was named to the See of Constantinople by the Emperor
Theodosius II. Nestorius seems to have been of a violent and
combative disposition. Setting out at once to be a strong leader,
he took strict measures against the remnants of the Arian heresy,

and against all suspect doctrines. Unfortunately, one of the doctrines he considered suspect was the teaching that the human and divine natures in Christ were so united that there are not two persons in Christ, but only one—the Divine Person of the Word—so that the Blessed Virgin Mary is truly called, not merely mother of Christ, but in a true sense Mother of God.

Nestorius had hardly been installed in Constantinople when he began to teach that there were not only two natures in Christ, but, in effect, two distinct persons. For him, the man Christ was only the temple, the vesture or garment of the God-head; and he made a sharp distinction between the actions of Christ's human nature and the actions of the Divine Person. In other words, he denied that the one Christ, the same Christ *is* both God and Man. He was thus led to repudiate, as a dangerous aberration, the title "Mother of God" as applied to the Blessed Virgin Mary.

The Nestorian teaching came almost immediately to the attention of Cyril, Patriarch of Alexandria, who had succeeded to that see in 412. Cyril, without mentioning Nestorius by name, preached against his doctrine at Easter, 429. Cyril of Alexandria was destined to be the great opponent of Nestorianism. Now Cyril himself is in many respects a controversial figure. The great defender of orthodoxy of his time, he nevertheless shared with Nestorius a certain ruthlessness and harshness of nature. And, more importantly from the standpoint of theology, some of Cyril's own terminology was, objectively at least, ambiguous, and was to be a focal point of post-Ephesian controversy leading to the Fourth General Council at Chalcedon in 451. The Nestorian controversy was to be complicated not only by the rivalry between the theological centers of Antioch and Alexandria, but also by the political rivalry between the ancient patriarchate of Alexandria, and the every increasing claims of power and eminence on the part of Constantinople, proud in its self-assumed title of the New Rome.

Very briefly, the events leading up to the Council of Ephesus proceeded in this fashion. Cyril defended the orthodox doctrine in a long letter to the monks of Egypt. Letters passed between Nestorius and Cyril demanding that Nestorius repudiate his teaching; Cyril being insistent, Nestorius being adamant. Both appealed to the Pope, Celestine I. The Pope called together a synod at Rome in August, 430. The synod upheld the position of Cyril and condemned that of Nestorius. Cyril was entrusted with conveying the condemnation to Nestorius, with the threat of deposition and excommunication unless he retracted. With the threat of an open and massive break looming in the Eastern Church, the Emperor, urged it would seem principally by Nestorius, summoned all the metropolitans of the Empire to Ephesus.

The bishops met on June 22, 431. Nestorius was there, with sixteen friendly bishops and an escort guard. Cyril arrived with a number of his suffragan bishops and a large lay entourage. When the session opened, neither the three legates of the Pope had yet arrived, nor John, the Patriarch of Antioch. Cyril, over the protests of the Captain of the Imperial Guard, who represented the Emperor, refused to delay the opening session. At the session, the Creed of Nicea was read first, then the famous *epistola dogmatica*, Cyril's second letter to Nestorius (Ep. 4), in which the Alexandrian had explained the traditional doctrine concerning the union of the two natures in one person in Christ. This letter was solemnly approved by the Fathers as being in complete accord with the faith of Nicea. The response of Nestorius was read and repudiated. Nestorius was proclaimed deposed and excommunicated. All this happened on the same day, June 22. We are told that the people of Ephesus, who had gathered before the church awaiting the decision, greeted it with a tremendous cry of joy. The bishops were escorted back to their lodgings with torches and burning incense. The streets and squares of the city flamed with light. It was like the civic celebration of a victory.

Nestorius protested to the Emperor; Cyril also sent a report. The irritated Emperor first reacted by deposing and imprisoning at Ephesus both Cyril and Nestorius, but they were soon released. John of Antioch arrived and gathered forty-three bishops in a counter-council and declared both Cyril and the Bishop of Ephesus deposed. The papal legates arrived and were present at the second, or July 10, session of the Council. They had been instructed by the Pope to adhere to and follow the lead of Cyril. Their letters from the Pope authoritatively called upon the Fathers of the Council to affirm and promulgate the Roman decision he had already forwarded to Cyril. On the eleventh of July, at the third session, the acts of the first day were read and approved by the papal legates. There was some further maneuvering, but the net result was victory for Cyril, who returned in triumph to Alexandria, and defeat for Nestorius, who retired to a monastery in Antioch.

We have said that the teaching of Nestorius would posit, in effect, two persons in Christ. But naturally his position was not expressed as simply as that. To supplement the extant fragments of Nestorius' writings, there was discovered in 1895 a Syriac translation of a work written by Nestorius late in life, justifying and elaborately explaining his teaching and severely criticizing the writings of Cyril and the decision of Ephesus. This work, the so-called "Book of Heraclides of Damascus" (the pseudonym was rendered necessary by the heresiarch's deposed and discredited status) abounds in orthodox terminology. Nestorius speaks of one Christ, one Son, etc. He is ever ready to speak of one person— but in his own particular sense. He writes that the divinity serves as person (personality) of the humanity, and the humanity serves as that of the divinity. In that sense we say that there is one person for them both.[7] While the "Book of Heraclides" has led some scholars (like Harnack, Loofs, Bethune-Baker, Duchesne) to tend to revise their opinion about the doctrine of Nestorius, Martin Jugie seems justified in adhering to the usual opinion. Jugie points out that even with the elaborate explanation and subtleties of the "Book of Heraclides," the fact remains that there is only an artificial, moral, voluntary union of the natures in Christ, not a physical, substantial one. Nestorius may well speak of "one Christ," etc., says Jugie, but each of these words provokes in the Nestorian thought-pattern the idea of two nature-persons, the divine and the human, which remain distinct.[8] And in spite

---

[7] Cf. Nestorius, *The Bazaar of Heracleides* (sic), trans. G. R. Driver and Leonard Hodgson (Oxford: Clarendon Press, 1925), p. 301.

[8] Cf. Martin Jugie, *Theologia Dogmatica Christianorum Orientalium*, Tome 4 (Paris: Letouzey et Ané, 1926).

of all the self-justification of Nestorius, he still will not say of God the Word that He was born of the Blessed Virgin.

Let the teaching which was approved (or rather reaffirmed as traditional) at Ephesus be stated in the words of the Letter of Cyril that was read there:

> . . . although (the Son) subsisted and was begotten of the Father before the worlds, He is spoken of as having been born also after the flesh of a woman: not that His divine nature had its beginning of existence in the Holy Virgin, or needed of necessity on its own account a second generation after its generation from the Father . . . but forasmuch as the Word having 'for us and for our salvation' personally united to Himself human nature came forth of a woman, for this reason He is said to have been born after the flesh. For He was not first born an ordinary man of the holy Virgin, and then the Word descended upon Him, but having been made one with the flesh from the very womb itself, He is said to have submitted to a birth according to the flesh, as appropriating and making His own the birth of His own flesh.

One last remark is offered on the doctrinal issues at Ephesus. While the repudiation of Nestorius' refusal to grant to the Virgin the title, "Mother of God," has placed the emphasis of the Council, at least popularly, on Mariology, it is quite clear that the heresy of Nestorius was directly Christological, and not Mariological; or rather, Mariological only by a necessity of consistency. The word at issue with regard to the Virgin was *theotókos,* from *theós* (God) and *tokos* (generation, or parturition). When Nestorius denied this title to our Lady, he was defying a long Christian tradition, a tradition to which Cyril appeals when he states:

> This is the doctrine which strict orthodoxy everywhere prescribes. Thus shall we find the Holy Fathers to have held. So did they make bold to call the Holy Virgin "the Mother of God" (*theotókos*). Not as though the nature of the Word or His Godhead had its beginning from the Holy Virgin, but forasmuch as His holy Body, imbued with a rational soul, was born of her, to which Body also the Word was personally united, on this account He is said to have been born after the flesh.

It is right that Ephesus should stand forever as a testimony before the world that to deny to Mary the title, "Mother of God," is to deny the true faith concerning Christ. *Theotókos* is not simply a word that may be taken or left alone. May I quote Newman once again:

> . . . the confession that Mary is *Deipara,* or the Mother of God, is that safeguard wherewith we seal up and secure the doctrine of the Apostle from all evasion, and that test whereby we detect all the pretenses of those bad spirits of "Anti-christs which have gone out into the world." It declares that He is God; it implies that He is man; it suggests to us that He is God still, though He has become man, and that He is true man though He is God. By witnessing to the *process* of the union, it secures the reality of the two *subjects* of the union, of the divinity and of the manhood. If Mary is the Mother of God, Christ must be literally Emmanuel, God with us . . . so now, and to the latest hour of the Church, do her glories and the devotion paid her proclaim and define the right faith concerning Him as God and man. Every church which is dedicated to her, every altar which is raised under her invocation, every image which represents her, every litany in her praise, every Hail Mary for her continual memory, does but remind us that there was One who, though He was all blessed from all eternity, yet for the sake of sinners, "did not shrink from the Virgin's womb."

And so it was (in brief and most inadequate summary) that the Holy Spirit guided the Church of God, so that in the fourth and fifth centuries of our era, in Nicea and Ephesus in Asia Minor, it might, through the voice of a general council, protect and defend and explain the Faith of Jesus Christ.

Very Reverend Edmond D. Bernard

The Return of Orthodox Christians:
The Council of Florence

The Return of Orthodox Christians:
The Council of Florence

THE PREPARATION of this study has been primarily an exercise in prudence. I mean Thomistic prudence: putting reason into virtue. The virtue lay in accepting the invitation of a distinguished university to treat the Council of Florence. The task of reason was to be intelligently and sincerely selective: to simplify and still not falsify, to omit and yet not sin by omission, to pass judgment on historical evidence and not on confessional prejudice.

I have limited this study to the theological issues at Florence. To cover these issues in so short a space, I am compelled to presuppose in my readers a fund of historical knowledge which may or may not exist. I must presuppose a background of schism: the Photian Schism of the ninth century, the Cerularean Schism of the eleventh; the Great Schism that sundered East and West, the schism within the Western Church from 1378 till 1417. I must presuppose a background of union: steps towards union at Lyons in 1274, at Constance in 1414, by Martin V till his death in 1431. I must presuppose the sheer history of the Council itself: its ten months in Ferrara, its four years in Florence, its undetermined span of life in Rome.[1] I must begin with the first doctrinal session on October 8, 1438; with the presence in Ferrara of some 360 Latin ecclesiastics (including Pope Eugenius IV) and 700 Greeks (including Emperor John VIII of Constantinople and Patriarch Joseph II of Constantinople). And I must be content to set before

---

[1] Also of high significance are the six turbulent years (1431-37) in Basel, before Eugenius IV transferred that Council to Ferrara on September 18, 1437. Those years and Basel's agenda are especially important for the problem of the relation between Pope and general council. Some scholars prefer to speak of the Council of Basel-Ferrara-Florence: e.g., Philip Hughes, *The Church in Crisis: A History of the Twenty Great Councils* (London, 1961), p. 241.

you the four doctrinal issues: the procession of the Spirit, purgatory, the Eucharist, and the primacy.[2]

The Nicene Creed—more accurately, the Niceno-Constantinopolitan Creed, the Creed of Nicea as developed by the First Council of Constantinople in 381—had declared of the Holy Spirit: "We believe . . . in the Holy Spirit . . . who proceeds from the Father *(to ek tou patros ekporeuomenon)*. . . ."[3] In seventh-century Spain an addition was made to this last cause, "who proceeds from the Father"; the clause now read "who proceeds from the Father and the Son." It was not till the beginning of the eleventh century that Rome introduced the phrase "and the Son." It was not that Rome doubted the doctrine; she did not. The problem was prudence: Was it advisable to alter the traditional form of words in so significant, so universal an expression of faith? In the eleventh century, Rome decided that it was advisable.

At the Council of Florence the first issue, and the main issue, was a single Latin word, *Filioque.* Perplexing perhaps, but not without precedent. In 325 Nicea had found its focus in a solitary Greek word, *homoousios;* in 431 Ephesus had centered on another Greek word, *theotokos;* in 1438-39 the word that divided the world was *Filioque.* In point of fact, the problem was two-pronged: one prong we may call procedural, the other substantive. These two facets of the *Filioque* problem, Florence debated separately, successively; for the Greeks declined to discuss the second before the first had been disposed of.

Procedural Problem

Fourteen sessions at Ferrara, from October 8 to December 13, 1438, dealt with the procedural problem: Was the addition, "and

---

[2] It will be apparent how deeply indebted I am to that remarkable synthesis of scholarly research, *The Council of Florence,* by Joseph Gill, S.J. (Cambridge, 1959). I have, however, worked from the documents themselves, and the translations, though profiting from Gill's versions, are largely my own.

[3] J. D. Mansi, *Sacrorum conciliorum nova et amplissima collectio* 3 (Florence, 1759), 565.

the Son," legitimate? Not legitimate in the sense of doctrinally correct; this issue was second on the agenda. The legitimacy in question came down to this: Is any alteration in the faith of Nicea justified? Is it legitimate to introduce any addition into the Nicene Creed?

The case for the Greeks was summarized in a single sentence by Mark, Metropolitan of Ephesus: ". . . we are going to speak about the addition made in the Creed, that it ought not to have been made and was utterly illegitimate; for this was the original reason for the schism."[4] Even more pointedly, when asked by Andrew of Rhodes: "If the addition is true, why not add it?" Mark retorted, "Because it is forbidden." The Greek case rested on a number of conciliar, patristic, and papal pronouncements, but predominantly on a prohibition of the Council of Ephesus in 431:

> When, therefore, these things had been read out, the holy Synod decreed that no one was permitted to put forward, that is, to write or compose, another faith than that which was laid down by the holy fathers assembled in the Holy Spirit at Nicea. Those who dared either to compose, that is, to produce, another faith, or to propose another faith to those desirous of turning to knowledge of the truth either from paganism or from Judaism or from any heresy whatever it be, such, if they were bishops or clerics, were to be alienated, bishops from the episcopacy, clerics from the clergy; but if laymen, they were to be excommunicated.[5]

The first Latin reply came from Andrew, Archbishop of Rhodes. Addition, Andrew insisted, is one thing; development, amplification, exposition, clarification is another. If addition is forbidden, development is not—not forbidden by the New Testament, not forbidden by the Fathers, not forbidden by the councils. Were it

---

[4] *Quae supersunt actorum graecorum Concilii Florentini,* ed. Iosephus Gill, S.I. (= *Concilium Florentinum: Documenta et scriptores,* ed. Pontificium Institutum Orientalium Studiorum, Series B, Vol. 5; Rome, 1953), p. 49. This volume is hereafter referred to as *Acta graeca.* For a prudent evaluation of the various sources, cf. Gill, *The Council of Florence,* pp. viii-xiv.—The Greek clause which I have translated "ought not to have been made" could be turned "was made without need"; but I do not think the latter version interprets the actual situation as pointedly as the former.

[5] *Acta graeca,* p. 69; cf. Mansi 4, 1361-1364; E. Schwartz, *Acta conciliorum oecumenicorum* 1, 1, 7 (Berlin-Leipzig, 1929), 105-106.

forbidden, the Church would be made impotent—quite powerless in the face of new crises, powerless to fulfill an inescapable function, her task of teaching. Now the *Filioque* is not an addition to the Creed; it is a development contained in *ex Patre*. Therefore, it is not forbidden.

The Greek rebuttal was voiced by Bessarion, Metropolitan of Nicea. Development is not forbidden; you are quite right. But it is forbidden to add to the Creed—forbidden to add even a word. Ephesus forbade not simply a profession of another faith; Ephesus forbade another profession of the same faith. And Ephesus obeyed its own injunction: it did not insert *theotokos* into the Creed, though the Creed contained *theotokos* in principle and the addition would have been highly useful in the Nestorian crisis. And no council since Ephesus has added to the Creed. The councils found another way: they left the Creed intact and they added definitions outside the Creed to meet the crisis of the moment.

> . . . we wish Your Reverence [Andrew of Rhodes] to know that we withhold this license [to add even a word to the Creed] from every Church and synod, even an ecumenical synod, and not from the Roman Church alone. However powerful the Roman Church may be, its power is less than an ecumenical synod or the universal Church. Since, therefore, we withhold this permission from the whole Church, so much the more do we withhold it from the Roman Church. We withhold it, however, not by our own authority; rather, we regard it as forbidden by the decrees of the fathers.[6]

It was in vain that the Latins, especially Cardinal Cesarini, argued that the intention of the legislators, the mind of Ephesus, was to outlaw only a profession of faith which differed in substance from the Symbol of Nicea. No, said the Greeks; the mind of Ephesus was to debar any addition, even verbal, to the Creed of Nicea. The plea of Metropolitan Mark to the Latins was as uncompromising as it was impassioned:

> This Symbol, dear fathers, this fair trust from our fathers assembled in our royal city, we demand back from you. Restore it, then, just

---

[6] *Acta graeca*, p. 159.

as you received it from us. If someone had entrusted you with a deposit, would you not have surrendered it as you received it? So then, restore too the Symbol of our fathers as you received it. It does not admit of addition; it does not admit of diminution. They have closed it and they have sealed it; those who dare to make changes therein are cast out, and those who fashion another besides it are laid under penalty. The addition of this single word strikes you as a small matter, of little account. If that is so, to remove it would cost little or nothing; indeed, it would prove of immense profit, for it would link all Christians together. In point of fact, what was done was a serious matter, of great consequence. We are not at fault, therefore, in making a great issue over it. It was added for prudential reasons; for the same reasons remove it, that you may take to your bosoms sundered brethren who value love so highly.[7]

From Mark's remarks alone we would conclude that on the procedural problem, the sheer addition of any word to the Creed of Nicea, no progress had been effected; Latin and Greek were as severed as ever; the cleavage was complete. But, strangely enough, the records reveal that many a Greek mind was shaken; Bessarion, above all, in a private letter confessed himself shattered by the reasoning of Cesarini.[8] Before Cesarini, Bessarion was unmoved: Ephesus had forbidden any and every addition to the Creed—not only falsehood but even truth. Cesarini's arguments convinced him that it is always legitimate for a council to add the truth to the Creed; "and we, after many days of intense study, could make no reply."[9]

But on December 13, 1438, concord seemed discouragingly remote. Nine months in Ferrara, and the Greeks were weary and without hope. The more insistent the Latins on introducing the substantive problem (the truth or falsity of the *Filioque*), the more disheartened and pessimistic were the Greeks. The *Greek Acts* are graphic on this point:

---

[7] *Ibid.*, p. 216. Gill translates the last sentence thus: "It was added in the exercise of mercy. . . ." (*The Council of Florence*, p. 163). I suggest that the Greek *di' oikonomian*, so difficult to render with a word, refers to a policy of prudence, of practical wisdom, rather than to the virtue of mercy.

[8] *Ad Alexium Lescarin Philanthropinum de processione Spiritus sancti* (PG 161, 321-403; cf. esp. cols. 340-341).

[9] *Ibid.*, col. 341.

So we Greeks began to chafe—not only the prelates but all the clerics as well, even the higher-ranking courtiers, and the entire gathering—and we said: "What on earth are we doing talking and listening to empty words? They are not likely to persuade us, nor we them; so, the sensible thing is to go back home."[10]

Nor was their discouragement merely theological. Many were touchingly homesick: this would be their second Christmas away from home and family. The Pope owed them five months' back pay. The winter was cold, rain-streaked. And the rumor was strong that the Council was to move from Ferrara to Florence, to being all over again all those tedious, obstinate debates, this time on the dogma, with Latins who were already boasting of their patristic arguments.

In this context of utter frustration, two developments were little short of miraculous: the Greeks agreed to discuss the theology of the procession of the Holy Spirit, and they acquiesced in the papal decision to transfer the Council from Ferrara to Florence. It was reason that prevailed. Their own Emperor, John VIII, made it quite clear that, unless they discussed the dogmatic issue, the sojourn of the Greeks in Italy would prove disastrous, theologically and financially—and more so for Constantinople than for Rome. And a full assessment of the economic and military situation made it apparent that in Florence, but not in Ferrara, could be found the peace and prosperity so desirable if theological discussion is to be irenic and fruitful. Yes, reason prevailed; but in that very human context of bafflement and nostalgia, of mental obstinacy and physical misery, it was highly improbable that so abstract a power as reason would prevail.

Substantive Problem

In March, 1439, eight public sessions were held in Florence on the procession of the Holy Spirit. The protagonists were two: for the Greeks, Mark of Ephesus once more; for the Latins, the Dominican Provincial of Lombardy, John of Montenero. The first five sessions were, in the main, a matter of textual criticism:

---

[10] *Acta graeca*, p. 217.

Whose texts of Basil and Epiphanius are the more accurate? The textual wrangle was not impertinent, for the patristic evidence was admittedly of high significance. It was not impertinent, but it was inconclusive. In Session 6, Mark argued from texts of Scripture like John 15:26 *(ho para tou patros ekporeuetai)*, from councils like Constantinople I *(to ek tou patros ekporeuomenon)*, and from Fathers like Cyril of Alexandria, to the uncompromising conclusion that the Holy Spirit does not proceed, does not have His existence, from the Son but only from the Father.

> By all these reasons [so reads Mark's conclusion] we prove that our way of thinking is in harmony with the Holy Scriptures and with our divine fathers and teachers; that we change or adulterate no facet of the God-given dogmas transmitted to us from the beginning; that we add nothing, we subtract nothing, we make no slightest innovation. Again we call on Your Charity and Honor: be of one mind with us and the divine fathers; recite nothing in the churches and receive nothing beyond what they have said; with this and this alone be content—so that saying and thinking the same, with one voice and one heart we may in perfect harmony glorify the Father, the Son, and the Holy Spirit, to whom is due all glory, honor, and worship forever and ever. Amen.[11]

In Sessions 6, 7, and 8, John of Montenero presented the Latin case. The declaration with which he closed Session 6 afforded the Greeks their first strong hope for union. John said in part:

> ... Perhaps ... you think we are affirming ... that there are two causes of the Holy Spirit. You need have no fear on this point. The Roman Church has never erred and does not err on this. There is only one cause of the Holy Spirit. The Father is the principle both of Son and Spirit, but the Son, identical in nature with the Father, receives also to be producer of the Spirit, in respect of the common nature he has with the Father, and so is with him the principle, numerically one, of the Procession of the Holy Spirit. There is then but one cause of the Spirit, not two.[12]

---

[11] *Ibid.,* p. 382.

[12] The paraphrase is Gill's, *The Council of Florence,* p. 212. For the text on which the paraphrase is based, cf. *Andreas de Santacroce, advocatus consistorialis: Acta latina Concilii Florentini,* ed. G. Hofmann, S.I. (= *Concilium Florentinum: Documenta et scriptores,* Series B, Vol. 6; Rome, 1955), pp. 195-196. This volume is hereafter referred to as *Acta latina.*

In the last two public sessions Montenero argued at length from the New Testament conception of the Spirit, from the Latin doctors held in respect by the early councils, and from the most impressive of the Greek Fathers, to the Latin belief: the Spirit is from Father and Son, and Father and Son are one only principle of the Spirit.

What reaction did Montenero's presentation produce among the Greeks? We have Bessarion's summation: "[The Latins] brought forward passages not only of the Western teachers, but just as many of the Eastern. . . . To these we had no answer at all to make, save that they are corrupt and have been corrupted by the Latins." But, confessed Bessarion, the Greeks had no books that would prove the Latin texts corrupt, no saints who spoke otherwise than those put forward. "From no quarter did we find a reasonable argument left to us; and so we kept silent."[13] George Scholarius, the "philosopher," concurred:

> But you all see that the Latins have contended brilliantly for their faith so that no one with a sense of justice has any reason to reproach them. . . . On our part nothing was said to them to which they did not manifestly reply with wisdom, magnanimity and truth, and we have no Saint at all who clearly contradicts them.[14]

And still Mark remained unshaken. The texts adduced by the Latins from the Latin Fathers he refused to recognize. They had not been translated into Greek and so could not be checked by the Greeks. They had not been approved by the early ecumenical councils. They must have been falsified. Why? Because the Holy Spirit does not proceed from the Son, and therefore the saints could not have said that He does!

At the close of the March disputations, the situation was basically this: the Latins were more disputatious than ever; the Greeks had never been more weary of dispute. In the circum-

---

[13] *Ad Alexium Lescarin* (PG 161, 357).

[14] From the speech *On the Need of Aiding Constantinople*, addressed to the Greeks by Scholarius in Florence; text translated by Gill (*The Council of Florence*, pp. 225-226) from *Oeuvres complètes de Gennade Scholarius*, ed. L. Petit, X. A. Sidéridès, and M. Jugie (8 vols.; Paris, 1928-1936) 1, 297-299. The text may also be found in *PG* 160, 385-437; our specific quotation, cols. 388-389.

stances it could hardly have been otherwise. Few of the Greeks were trained theologians: even the best of them, like Mark, were content with quotations from their authorities and a minimum of commentary. Philosophy was not their forte; in fact, metaphysics in the service of theology they mistrusted mightily. That is why, as Father Gill observes,

> . . . Montenero's display of metaphysical niceties, his disquisitions on *substantia prima* and *secunda* and the philosophy of generation and the rest, far from clarifying the thoughts of most of his Greek hearers (and perhaps of not a few of the Latins too), would have served only to mystify them the more and to make them cleave the more tenaciously to their sheet-anchor in trinitarian theology—'from the Father alone'—feeling that Latin thought on the Blessed Trinity was far removed from the simple tradition they had inherited.[15]

When Montenero appealed to the authority of Aristotle, a Georgian envoy retorted: "What about Aristotle, Aristotle? A fig for your fine Aristotle." When asked what *is* fine, he replied: "St. Peter, St. Paul, St. Basil, Gregory the Theologian; a fig for your Aristotle, Aristotle."[16]

And yet an impression had been made on the Greeks—on two counts, each of which promised some sort of harmony with their own cherished ways of thinking. First, Montenero insisted that ultimately even the West held fast to *one* principle of the Holy Spirit; and second, the structure of Western belief was built on patristic thought, including the Greek Fathers in the original Greek. And it was a new experience, a shocking experience, for them to hear so many of their own Greek Fathers speak of the Spirit "proceeding from both," "issuing from both," "proceeding through the Son," even "being from the Son." It was startling to look in vain for a single Father who would say unequivocally "from the Father alone."

---

[15] Gill, *The Council of Florence*, p. 229.

[16] Translated by Gill (*ibid.*, p. 227) from the *Memoirs* written in Greek (not later than 1444) by Silvester Syropoulus, a deacon and official of the Great Church of Constantinople, who came to Italy in the entourage of Patriarch Joseph II and was an eyewitness of (at times an active participant in) what took place. The *Acta graeca,* the *Acta latina,* and the *Memoirs* are the three principal documents for the history and theology of Florence. The text is translated from the edition by R. Creyghton, *Vera historia unionis non verae* (The Hague, 1660) x, 12, p. 270.

Not that this was enough to turn the tide; it was not. After all, Scripture, through St. John, makes it indisputably clear that the Spirit "proceeds from the Father"; Scripture says nothing in express fashion on the procession from the Son. Montenero's "many Greek authorities had made them feel uneasy, but as yet had not persuaded them to abandon what they thought was the tradition of their Church, and they probably experienced the feeling that simpler folk commonly have when faced with a display of erudition, that did they but know a little more about the subject they could readily find an answer."[17]

Till the last week of May, 1439, the prospects for union were indeed dark. Three episodes prove it. First, on April 10 the Greeks sent the following message to Pope Eugenius:

> We are having no more public disputations, seeing that disputation produces nothing save irritation. For, whenever we say anything, you are never at a loss for an answer—at great length. And as we listen to what you say—arguments that are endless—who can go on listening and answering endlessly? Therefore, do you take counsel to see whether there is any other way of achieving union, and let us know of it. If there is no such way, we have said as much as we can. What we hold fast to is the faith we have inherited from our fathers, the faith transmitted by the seven synods; and this is enough for us.[18]

Second, another way leading towards union was tried, and it failed. Ten Latin and ten Greek delegates met in four or five private conferences, to uncover in this fashion some ground of agreement; but the private conferences, like the public, broke down. Third, at the request of the Greeks the Latins sent them a statement for their approval. In substance, the statement affirmed that the Greek formula "the Holy Spirit proceeds from the Father" does not intend to exclude the Son, that the Greeks "refrained from saying that the Holy Spirit proceeds from the Father and the Son because [the Greeks] thought that the Latins say that the Holy Spirit proceeds from the Father and the Son as from two principles and two spirations." And the statement went on to say that the Latin doctrine did not intend to exclude the Father "from

---

[17] Gill, *The Council of Florence*, p. 230.
[18] *Acta graeca*, p. 403.

being the source and principle of the whole of divinity"; that the procession of the Spirit from the Son does not mean "that the Son has not this from the Father, nor thereby do we assert that there are two principles or spirations." And the statement concluded with the affirmation that the patristic expression "from the Father through the Son" "is directed to this sense that by it is meant that the Son like the Father is according to the Greeks the cause, but according to the Latins the principle, of the subsistence of the Holy Spirit."[19] To this the Greeks returned an amended statement which in its theology of procession was deliberately ambiguous. When the Latins demanded a clarification of the ambiguities, the Greeks would not give it; the Emperor John VIII replied bluntly: "We write nothing else, we say nothing else, except this: If you accept what we have given, we will be united; if not, we shall go home."[20]

If we may speak of a turning point, it was May 27. With the consent of the Emperor, Pope Eugenius addressed an extraordinary session of all the Latin and Greek delegates. He recalled his initial high hopes, born of Greek enthusiasm and sacrifice; his growing disheartenment, shaped by delays in Ferrara and the cessation of debate in Florence; his profound sadness as he saw only disunion and wondered "what use to you [Greeks] division will be."

> . . . I exhort you, brethren . . . let there not be division in the Church of God. . . . Our union will procure rich profit for the soul; our union will bring high honor to the body; our union will dismay our enemies corporeal and incorporeal; our union will gladden the saints and the angels—there will be great joy in heaven and on earth.[21]

Somehow the Pope's appeal touched a responsive chord. The Greeks met together again to restudy the Fathers; and here hope burgeoned—burgeoned from a theological conviction dear to the

---

[19] Our extracts are borrowed from Gill, who has given an English version (*The Council of Florence*, pp. 247-248) of this *cedula* on the basis of Syropoulus' *Memoirs* (Creyghton viii, 13, p. 235-16, p. 247), the *Acta latina* (pp. 224, 254), and the Decree of Union (*Acta graeca*, pp. 461-462.

[20] *Acta graeca*, p. 420.

[21] *Ibid.*, pp. 423-424.

Greek mind. The conviction was: the saints cannot err in matters of faith; they are inspired by the same Spirit, and so they
must agree. Now the saints of both Churches had written much
on the Trinity: Latin saints said that the Spirit proceeds from
Father and Son; Greek saints said that the Spirit proceeds, bursts
forth, issues from the Father, from the Father through the Son,
from both. Therefore, since the saints must agree, the different
expressions must ultimately mean the same thing; the discrepancy
can only be apparent; it cannot be real.

In this context there was but one way to attack the orthodoxy
of the Latin doctrine, and that was to accuse the Latins of forging
their Latin Fathers. This is precisely what Mark of Ephesus did—
to the end. His prestige, personal and professional, was high;
but he made no effort to prove his case. (How could he? He
knew no Latin.) Gradually Greek opposition ebbed, and by
June 8 the vast majority had subscribed to a formula of faith no
different from the formula they had frowned on a month before
and altered to ambiguity.

Agreement on the procession of the Spirit meant that reunion
was no longer a dream: the crucial cleavage in doctrine had
disappeared. But before reunion could be utter reality, several
other doctrinal issues had to be resolved; and this was the task
of the month that lay ahead. For the Latins were convinced that
union would be chimerical unless harmony were reached on
purgatory, on the Eucharist, and on the primacy.

PURGATORY

Purgatory had been warmly debated in informal sessions in
Ferrara.[22] Much of the dissension centered on purgatorial fire,
which the Greeks were unwilling to admit. The Ferrara discussions revealed a vexing vagueness among the Greek prelates on
what the Greek Church acutally taught in regard to man's destiny
after death. Some of the positions advanced were of a nature to
shock the West. Take Metropolitan Mark's summary: Neither
the just nor the wicked will attain to their final state before the

---

[22] Cf. Gill, *The Council of Florence,* pp. 117-125.

the Last Judgment. In the meantime the just do not enjoy the direct vision of God; their happiness consists in hope, which is as proper to their state as faith is proper to earth-bound mortals and charity to heaven's souls after the Judgment. The reprobate will not be punished by fire till after the Last Day; then as now their primary pain will be loss. Those in the middle state, guilty at death of minor faults, are punished in varying degrees in proportion to their guilt; one penalty is uncertainty of the hour of release; another, the shame or sense of guilt. Mark did not admit a debt of temporal punishment due to sins already forgiven.

With this background in Ferrara, it is not surprising to hear Cardinal Cesarini tell the Latins in Florence: "the problems were so many that I all but despaired." Fortunately, however, Cesarini could go on to say: "at long last, by God's action, the Greeks now admit the truth" that those who die in charity but either with venial sin unremitted or with penance to perform go to purgatory, that the wicked go to hell and the just to heaven immediately after death. As for the vision of God, this point almost doomed the delegates to defeat; but at length the Greeks "yielded to argument and recognized that the souls of the blessed will see God, Three and One, just as He is."[23]

EUCHARIST

Two facets of the Eucharist were debated in Florence: matter and form.[24] The question of matter caused little concern. The Greeks used leavened, fermented bread; the Latins used unleavened, unfermented bread; and some of the Greeks would have liked to see unfermented bread forbidden. But the vast majority agreed that here they confronted sheer custom, of no great consequence; that whether the bread was fermented or unfermented, leavened or unleavened, mattered not a whit as long as the bread was wheaten.

The question of form threatened to be difficult. For the Latins looked with apprehension on the Greek epiklesis. They wanted

[23] *Acta latina*, pp. 254-255.
[24] Cf. Gill, *The Council of Florence*, pp. 272-286, 292-293.

assurance from the Greeks that the epiklesis, "May it become the body and blood of Christ," did not displace or diminish the words of institution, "This is my body," as effectuating transubstantiation; and they wanted this written into the formula of union, into the definition. The Greeks replied that their doctrine on the form of the Sacrifice had never differed from the Latin; they claimed that to include this item in the definition would be to discredit their past; they pointed out that even the Latin Mass prays after the Consecration "Bid that these offerings be carried by the hands of thy holy angel to thy altar on high." Fortunately for union, the Greeks persuaded the Latins to be content with an oral declaration to the effect that it is our Lord's words of institution that transubstantiate bread and wine into the body and blood of Christ.

PRIMACY

Papal primacy, too, deadlocked the delegates.[25] The criterion accepted by both sides was that such privileges as had been demonstrably enjoyed by the popes, from the beginning and before the schism should still be recognized. The Latins argued from Scripture, from the Fathers, and from the councils that the Roman Pontiff is the successor of Peter, vicar of Christ, head of the whole Church, father of all Christians, teacher of Christendom, with a primacy over the whole world, that to the Roman See and to the Roman Pontiff in St. Peter was given plenary power to feed, convene, rule, and govern the whole Church. Greek objections from history, tradition, and theology were countered by Montenero, who insisted that the Pope enjoyed authority and not merely respect, that his was a spiritual jurisdiction directed to the salvation of all Christians, that his power was monarchic, immediate, and universal. The Greeks were not yet convinced. At one point the Emperor gave up all hope and bluntly told the Pope's emissaries: "Make arrangements for our departure, if you will be so kind."[26] Ultimately, however, they yielded; they sent to Eugenius this acceptable formula:

---

[25] Cf. *ibid.*, pp. 272-274, 278-282, 284, 286.
[26] *Acta graeca*, p. 452.

About the primacy of the Pope, we confess that he is supreme pontiff, representative and guardian and vicar of Christ, shepherd and teacher of all Christians, that he directs and governs the Church of God, without infringement of the privileges and rights of the patriarchs of the East: the patriarch of Constantinople second after the Pope, then the patriarch of Alexandria, the patriarch of Antioch after him, then the patriarch of Jerusalem.[27]

In the context of these successful negotiations—on purgatory, on the Eucharist, and on the primacy—it will not come as a surprise that the procedural issue on the procession of the Spirit was settled: the Synod would proclaim that *Filioque* had been lawfully added to the Creed.

UNION

The day of union was Monday, July 6, 1439.[28] Florence was festive, on holiday. The cathedral was crowded to its doors; the piazza outside was packed. The Greeks were on the epistle side, the Latins on the gospel side, the Emperor on his throne, when Pope Eugenius entered in procession, donned his Mass vestments, and sat down. Two by two, all the prelates, Latin and Greek, came forward to kiss his knee and his hand. Pontifical Mass followed, with the Epistle and Gospel read in Latin and Greek. At the close of Mass the papal faldstool was set centrally before the

---

[27] *Ibid.*, p. 453. A careful presentation of, and impressive reflection on, the primacy debate in Florence may be found in Gill's "The Definition of the Primacy of the Pope in the Council of Florence," *Heythrop Journal* 2 (1961), 14-29. From his study of the evidence he concludes that the Latins put before the Greeks not a minimalist but a maximalist interpretation of the primacy, with "no deception, no understatement" (p. 26); that the Greeks "brought a Greek and not a Latin mentality to their appreciation of the question" (*ibid.*), a preoccupation with the Roman *Church* rather than with the Pope, and a consequent stressing of the jurisdictional authority of the Holy See to the neglect of its teaching authority; that the Greeks did not quite realize that the teaching authority of the popes was being taught by the decree on the primacy; that the primacy was for the Greeks a canonical rather than a doctrinal issue. "What they could not fail to understand . . . was that the Roman Church was, not the equal, but the head of the other churches, because founded on St. Peter, the Christ-appointed head of the Apostles; that it had a universal jurisdiction and was therefore a court of appeal from all the world. If the dissident Churches of the East would now accept as much as did their fathers at Florence, the end of the schism would be in sight, for the transition from 'Roman Church' to 'Roman pope' would not be insuperable" (p. 29).

[28] Cf. Gill, *The Council of Florence*, pp. 293 ff.

altar; there Eugenius intoned the *Veni Creator Spiritus.* From a pulpit near the faldstool Cardinal Cesarini read the Decree of Union in Latin; Metropolitan Bessarion read the same Decree in Greek. Here, in digest form, is the Decree *Laetentur caeli* which resounded through the Florence cathedral that sixth day of July, 1439:

Eugenius, bishop, servant of God's servants:

Let the heavens rejoice, and earth leap for joy; for the wall that divided the Churches of East and West has been removed; peace and harmony have returned. Let Mother Church be gladsome; she who wept bitter tears over her children in their separation, let her thank God in joy for their wondrous harmony. Let all the faithful show joy, all through the world.

In the name of the Holy Trinity, Father, Son, and Holy Spirit, We define, with the approval of this universal Council, that the Holy Spirit is eternally from the Father and the Son, that He has His essence and His subsistent existence from Father and Son together, that He proceeds eternally from both as from one principle and one only spiration.

We define that the explanation *Filioque* was added to the Creed legitimately and for good reasons.

We define that the body of Christ is made truly present in wheaten bread, whether this be leavened or unleavened.

We define that the souls of those who die in God's love, truly repentant but without having satisfied for what they have done and left undone by fruits worthy of penance, are purified after death by cleansing punishments, and once purified are thereupon received into heaven and contemplate clearly God Himself, Three and One, just as He is.

We define that the holy Apostolic See and the Roman Pontiff hold primacy over the whole world; that the same Roman Pontiff is successor of blessed Peter, true vicar of Christ, head of the whole Church, father and teacher of all Christians; that to him in Peter our Lord Jesus Christ has delivered full power to feed, rule, and govern the universal Church.[29]

---

[29] The Latin and Greek texts of the Decree of Union may be found in *Acta graeca,* pp. 459-464. My translation is made on the Latin text. For practical reasons, I have given only a digest of the Decree, i.e., the actual words of the Decree, but omitting words, phrases, sentences, and even whole paragraphs. What remains is the essence of the doctrinal pronouncements on the major theological issues.

When Cesarini finished, Eugenius replied, "Placet"; the Latin prelates echoed, "Placet." When Bessarion finished, Emperor John VIII replied, "Agreed"; the Greeks present echoed, "Agreed." At that solemn moment the Greek Church and the Latin Church were one—one Church in faith. The schism was ended.

But the end of this schism was not the end of this Council. The Greeks went home, but Florence went on. In November, 1439, the Council received into union the Armenians of the Black Sea area; the pertinent Decree (the Degree for the Armenians) is perhaps particularly significant for its long section on the sacraments. In February, 1442, the Council received into union the Copts of Egypt; the pertinent Decree (the Decree for the Jacobites) presents in great detail Trinitarian and Christological doctrine. In February, 1443, Pope Eugenius transferred the Council to the Lateran Basilica in Rome. In September, 1444, the Council received into union the Syrians of Mesopotamia; here the three points of orthodoxy at issue were the procession of the Spirit, the two natures in Christ, and the two wills in Christ. Finally, in August, 1445, the Council received into union a small group of Chaldeans and Maronites on the island of Cyprus; the pertinent Bull stresses the procession of the Spirit, the constitution of Christ, and the seven sacraments. Sometime after the reception of the Cypriots, August 7, 1445, and before the death of Eugenius, February 23, 1447, the Council of Ferrara-Florence-Rome (or Ferrara-Florence-Lateran) came to a close.

DISUNION

There is a tragic epilogue: the union between the Greek and Latin Churches lasted less than fourteen years. The reasons are too intricate for simple analysis here.[30] We know that the masses of Constantinople—the man in the street and the monk, the lower clergy and the nuns—were hostile to union from the beginning.

---

[30] Cf. Gill, *The Council of Florence,* chapter 10: "The Reception of the Union in the East" (pp. 349-388). There are, of course, many important studies on the immediate and remote aftermath of Florence; a recent contribution is Oscar Halecki's *From Florence to Brest (1439-1596)* (Rome, 1958).

Mark of Ephesus and George Scholarius, influential leaders both, conducted a steady campaign of propaganda against it in a city sympathetic to their cause. No comparable campaign to defend the union was waged either by the Emperor, for all his ecclesiastical authority, or by the Pope. Anti-Latinism was a centuries-old constituent of Greek character. Even with the Turks an imminent threat, opposition to union could be expressed in the cry, "Better to see the turban of the Turk ruling in the midst of the city than the Latin mitre." Constantinople's appeal to the West for help against the Sultan's siege evoked relatively small response. But even had military aid been massive, it is doubtful that it would have daunted the crowds who roamed the city shouting, "We don't want Latin help or Latin union; let us be rid of the worship of the unleavened." Whatever the reasons, the fact is that on May 29, 1453, Constantinople fell to the Turks, and with it fell the union of Florence.

One last question: What of the charge, made then as now, that the Greeks did not enter into union freely? We do have reason to believe that a number of the prelates who signed the Decree of Union in Florence repudiated their signatures in Constantinople. But why did they sign in the first place? Did they (as was soon suggested) sell their signatures? Were they browbeaten by the Emperor? Did nostalgia and hunger and depression ravish their freedom? I submit that the extant evidence bears out the conclusion reached by Father Gill in a recent article:

> No. The Greek prelates in Florence were free and freely accepted the doctrine of the *Filioque* and the other doctrines, and freely united with the Latins. To say that they betrayed their faith because of some not very terrible inconveniences is to condemn them as cowards and to cast an aspersion on the whole of the Greek Church of that day whose highest ecclesiastics, except for two, would have to be said to have accepted what to them was heresy, because the alternative was, not martyrdom or even exile, but a rather protracted absence from home. That is a condemnation that is too scathing, and it is not true. The historical sources give a different picture. They portray a group of men of different intellectual capabilities. There was a minority of able theologians, all of whom except one were convinced of the orthodoxy of the Latin faith and the soundness of the union—and

not one of these changed his opinion later. The rest, less capable theologians and so more liable to be influenced by circumstances, acclaimed Latin doctrine and union in Florence, when their own theologians produced convincing reasons and the atmosphere of the Council fostered unity, and began to doubt and to repent of their previous action in Constantinople, when the monks and mob assailed them and the atmosphere of the city was hostile to unity. These were not dishonest men. They were men whose sentiment was stronger than their intellects and they were, perhaps, not cast in an heroic mould.[31]

Very Reverend Walter J. Burghardt, S.J.

---

[31] Joseph Gill, "The Council of Florence (1438-1439): A Success That Failed," *Month,* n.s. 23 (1960), 210.

The Reform of the Church
and the Council of Trent

The Reform of the Church and
the Council of Trent

THE FATHERS of the Council of Trent on Saturday, December 4, 1563,[1] had been in public session for two consecutive days, something that had happened never before in the annals of the great assembly. And now, in this, its twenty-fifty session, the ninth of its third convocation, after all the crises, all the deadlocks that more than once had threatened a collapse in failure; after having been twice suspended and reconvened, the Council brought its gigantic labors to an end.[2]

On the first day, December 3, the Fathers passed the decrees on purgatory, on the invocation of saints, and the veneration of relics; they promulgated the important decrees on the reform of the religious orders and a score of other laws of canonical discipline affecting all the estates of the Church from the cardinals down to the secular magistrates. The hour grew late, and they continued the session to the next day, when they passed a brief decree on feasts and fasts, and one on indulgences, entreating all bishops to abolish every abuse, suppress all that savors superstition and filthy lucre—a final reminder, as it were, of the scandals that had triggered the Lutheran revolution almost half a century be-

---

[1] This lecture was delivered on December 4, 1961.

[2] The decrees and the concluding ceremonies of Session 25 are found in *Canones et decreta sacrosancti oecumenici et generalis Concilii Tridentini sub Paulo III, Julio III, Pio IV, Pontificibus maximis,* first (official) edition, Rome, 1564, frequently reprinted. For a recent text (based on the edition of Naples, 1859) with English translation, see H. J. Schroeder, O.P., *Canons and Decrees of the Council of Trent* (St. Louis and London, 1941), pp. 215 ff., 482 ff. The full minutes are in the *Acta,* ed. S. Ehses in *Concilium Tridentinum: Diariorum, actorum, epistularum, tractatuum nova collectio* ed. Societas Goerresiana [hereafter cited as CT], vol. 9 (Freiburg, 1924), 1076-1098, 1111-1120.

91

fore. Then, after deciding to turn over the unfinished business of
the Index, and of the reform of catechism, breviary, and missal to
the Roman Pontiff, the Council resolved that the time had come
to disband, for the bishops could no longer stay away from their
flocks; they went on record to state that there was no longer any
hope that the Protestants would arrive, although they had been so
often invited, so often been granted the safe-conduct they had
requested. All the decrees and definitions of the preceding sessions were once more recited (This lengthy business had been one
of the main reasons why two days had been set aside for the closing session). This done, the presiding legate, Cardinal Morone,
asked the Fathers for a vote as to whether it was their pleasure to
put an end to this holy ecumenical Council; and whether it was
their pleasure that the legates should request from the Roman
Pontiff confirmation of each and all that had been decreed in it?
And they replied, "It so pleases" *(Placet)*. Whereupon the
legate-president, blessing the assembly, said, "Go in peace."

"And then," we read[3] in the official transcript of the aging
Bishop Angelo Massarelli, who had been the Council's Secretary
over all these long, long years—we almost see his hand tremble
as he sets down the phrase—"and then the most illustrious and
most reverend Lord Cardinal of Lorraine cried with loud voice
the words written below, to wit:

> "To the most blessed Pius, our Lord, Pontiff of the holy universal
> Church, many years and eternal memory."
> Response of the Fathers: "O God, do Thou preserve the Holy Father
> very long to Thy Church, many years."
> Cardinal: "To the souls of the Supreme Pontiffs, Paul III and Julius
> III, by whose authority this holy general council was begun: peace
> from the Lord and eternal glory and happiness in the light of the
> saints."
> Response: "Be their memory in benediction."

And so forth; there follow the liturgical acclamations: for the
late Emperor Charles V, Emperor Ferdinand, the Christian kings,
nations, and princes, the papal legates, the cardinals, and ambas-

---

[3] *Sess.* 25, *Acclamationes patrum.* I have departed in some points from
Schroeder's translation, p. 257 f.

sadors, for the bishops and for the holy assembly itself; there
follow the invocations of our Lady and all saints, and the final
anathema of all heretics; all those set formulae of acclamatory
chant from the *ordo* of the ancient councils, which in turn were
only a continuance of the ritual of the Roman Senate (the bishops
at Trent themselves being significantly acclaimed "to the heralds
of truth, perpetual memory, to the orthodox senate, many years")
. . . and all this intoned by Charles Guise, the Cardinal of Lorraine, who only a few months ago had been the protagonist of
the conciliar opposition.

The moving scene is followed by an anticlimactic, dry notice in
the official record: "After this the presiding legates commanded
all fathers under pain of excommunication that before leaving the
city of Trent they must sign the decrees by their own hand . . .
and they all signed, 255 in number, i.e., 4 legates, 2 cardinals,
3 patriarchs, 25 archbishops, 168 bishops, 7 abbots, 39 proctors of
those absent, with lawful commission, 7 generals of orders."

A few weeks later, Pope Pius IV confirmed the decrees in con-
sistory, January 26, 1564—against the last-minute opposition of
certain powerful circles in Rome.[4]   Indeed, once the Pope would
put his seal, "I Pius, Bishop of the Catholic Church," under the
document of confirmation, he thereby would ratify and give the
force of universal law also to conciliar enactments which in so
many respects ran counter to the time-honored practices and
prerogatives that hid behind the elegant name of *stylus Curiae;*
conciliar enactments which expressly had not only included the
cardinals in their measures of reform but even entreated the Pope
in these words:[5]

> Finally, this holy Council, moved by so many grave afflictions of the
> Church, cannot but call to mind that the holy Roman Pontiff should
> apply that solicitude which he owes the universal church by duty of

---

[4] Pius IV, *Bulla super confirmatione,* appended to the *Canones et decreta* (English text in Schroeder, pp. 268-273). For the opposition see P. Richard, *Concile de
Trente* (Hefele-Leclercq, *Histoire des Conciles,* vol. 9; Paris, 1931) pp. 995 ff.
The Pope's displeasure with it can be seen from his consistorial addresses of
December 30, 1563, (cf. CT 9.1143, lines 24-25) and January 26, 1564, (*ibid.*
1151, lines 22-24): no cardinal should hereafter dare to propose anything against
the decrees; no damage the Curia might seem to suffer is to be taken into account.
[5] *Sess.* 24, *de reform.* c.1 (italics mine).

his office, *in a special way* by associating with himself as cardinals the most select persons only, and appoint to each bishopric good and competent shepherds ... because Jesus Christ will require from his hands the blood of His sheep that perish through the bad government of careless shepherds. ...

It is to the lasting credit of Pius IV that he did not listen to those who tempted him to use his sovereign authority to modify the Tridentine decrees and to avail himself of the clause "without prejudice to the authority of the Holy See" which the Fathers had appended to them in their last session.[6]

That was December 4, 1563.—Now let us draw the curtain over the jubilant last scene and follow the memories of the few protagonists who had lived to witness both the beginning and the closing of the Council—the quiet Secretary, Massarelli, being one of them—to the hour of the solemn opening session eighteen years earlier on December 13, 1545, with Pope Paul III's three cardinal legates officiating; with only thirty-one bishops and five superiors general of religious orders present as voting members.[7] Ominously, only one bishop from Germany, the nation most concerned, was among them and he but a titular bishop, proctor for his Ordinary, the Cardinal Archbishop Elector of Mainz; and he stayed for the first two sessions only. It was Gaudete Sunday, and the sermon of the day was preached by the bishop of Bitonto on that verse of the Introit. Rereading the sermon today in the Acts of the Council, with its stately rhetoric and its flattery for the cardinals,[8] we cannot but think that in the minds of the Fathers present, the call to "Rejoice in the Lord" met with the anxious question whether the Council, at long last assembled, a quarter of a century after the seamless garment of the Church had been rent, did not come too late to fulfill its mission.

A deep insight into the mood of the Council, much deeper than from the festive oratory of the first day, will be gained from the

---

[6] *Sess.* 25, *de reform.* c.21. Pius IV announced he was going to change nothing: CT 9.1143, lines 21-22; p. 1144, lines 16-19 (where the phrase, ". . . it is a word worthy of the supreme ruler [*princeps*] if he professes to be bound by the law" is an implied quotation from Justinian's *Codex,* 1.14.4, not recognized by the editor).

[7] Cf. *Acta,* CT 4, ed. Ehses (1904), list of prelates present, pp. 529-532.

[8] CT 4.521-29.

Admonitio of the cardinal legates, read on their behalf by the Secretary of the Council in the second session, January 7, 1546. The document[9] had been composed by the English cardinal, Reginald Pole, the prelate whom his royal cousin Henry VIII persecuted with unremitting hatred. Pole belonged to that group of deeply religious, selfless men of apostolic spirit whom Paul III, breaking with the sad traditions of the Renaissance popes, had raised to the cardinalate in 1536 and who embodied that new ideal of the saintly and learned cleric in high places which was the hope of the best for a regeneration, not only of the Sacred College but of the Church at large in those fateful years.

What the *Admonitio* had to say was strong medicine for many. It was all the more impressive because of the classical simplicity of its style, nurtured in the language of Scripture and the Fathers, and because of the sincerity and urgency of its thought. I must resist the temptation to quote (and to quote in the admirable Latin prose of the original) more from it than a few excerpts. The document starts out from the threefold purpose of the Council as it had been laid down in Pope Paul's bull of convocation and in the formal decree of Session I: extirpation of heresies—reformation of ecclesiastical discipline and morals—peace of the Church.

> We must exhort all here assembled, but first *of all we must exhort ourselves* who preside over this sacred council, never to give room to the thought that we as individuals or as a universal assembly—even if all shepherds of the whole world were gathered here—could heal all the ills that now burden Christ's flock. For if we think that we, or any one else but Christ Himself, to whom the Father has given all power, could accomplish this, then we shall err in the very foundation of all our endeavors, and shall call down on ourselves the wrath of God.[10]

Pole goes on to compare all human counsel that does not come from the breathing of the Holy Spirit, to the wells of which the prophet Jeremiah says that they cannot contain the torrents of liv-

---

[9] *Ibid.*, 548-553. For Pole's authorship see Ehses, *ibid.* 548, n.2.
[10] *Ibid.*, 549, lines 5-10 (italics mine).

ing water.[11] Only if we are aware of our own insufficiencies, shall we be fit. "If we want to tell the truth we must say that we are conscious of having failed in our ministry and that in no small degree *we ourselves have been the cause of the evils* which now we are called upon to correct; it is not enough to say that we are not equal to so great a burden."[12] We must do, Pole says, what Christ Himself did, Who took upon Himself the atonement for all our sins as though He had committed what we committed. "Justice itself demands that we, the shepherds, put ourselves as culprits before God's tribunal for the ills of our flocks and implore His mercy through Jesus Christ. . . ."[13]

It is no rhetorical exaggeration (Pole goes on) to say that we are the cause of these evils. The heresies are first. We certainly have not originated them; but if they could grow in the field of God, the care of which has been entrusted to us, is not the negligent farmer who did not till the fields as much at fault as he who sowed the cockle? Next is the decay of ecclesiastical discipline and the abuses. Here one does not have to search long to find who is the source of this evil, *because except for our own persons we could name no other source.* Third is the lack of peace. Again the *Admonitio* insists on "our ambitions, our avarice, our cupidity" as the cause of why the tribulations have come.[14]

"Why do we say all this? To embarrass you? Far be it, but rather because we want to admonish you, and to admonish ourselves in the first place, to do everything that we may avoid the terrible judgment of God. . . ."[15]

I must forego further quotations from what the *Admonitio* has to say to bishops, to the Christian princes, and especially to the bishops who have come to the Council with mandates and instructions from their sovereigns. It concludes with some thoughts on the spirit of peace in which the Fathers of the Council should conduct their discussions and once more underlines the great task before them: "In all that pertains to the reformation of the

---

[11] Jerem. 2.13.
[12] CT 4.549, lines 31-35 (italics mine).
[13] *Ibid.*, lines 37 ff., 46-50.
[14] *Ibid.*, lines 51 ff.; p. 550, lines 9 ff., 24 ff., 44 (italics mine).
[15] *Ibid.*, 551, lines 1-4.

Church, *for which purpose we are here assembled,* let us imitate Him Who first formed the Church. . . ."[16] And then, we read in Massarelli's record, *"cum paululum omnes quievissent"* (after all had rested a little while),[17] the session turned to the business of the day.

I hope these excerpts will convey the deep concern with the theme of reform of oneself which pervades the whole document. Time and again Pole stresses the responsibility of the Council for bringing about a genuine regeneration of Christian life, so much so that the task of eradictating the great heresies of the times is seen, in the first place, as a challenge for *positive* work in tilling the field of God, for fulfilling one's task rather than holding responsible the sower of the cockle. This, I think, is a point that should be stressed in an over-all appreciation of the work of Trent.

It is commonly known that the Decrees of Trent consist in part of extremely important dogmatic definitions of Catholic truths, and in part of measures of disciplinary reform. The summary of the dogmatic definitions was, after the conclusion of the Council, to be formulated by Pope Pius IV (November 15, 1564) in the so-called Tridentine profession of faith, the same to which we solemnly pledge ourselves by an oath at the beginning of each academic year. But this condensed formula cannot possibly give us an adequate idea of the tremendous labors that had been spent in the carefully reasoned exposition of each and every truth which we now read summarized in this profession of faith. In some instances, the teaching of the Council even defies such a brief summarization; for example, when we profess: "all and everything the holy Synod of Trent has defined and declared concerning original sin and justification I embrace and accept."

In "defining and declaring," the teaching Church assembled at Trent did not content itself with condemning heretical propositions; and, in striking contrast with many earlier councils, it abstained altogether from a condemnation of the persons of the innovators; the names of Luther, Zwingli, Calvin, etc., do not appear in the anathemas that were appended to each of the dog-

---

[16] *Ibid.,* 553, lines 24-25 (italics mine).
[17] *Ibid.,* line 42.

matic decrees in the time-hallowed form, "If any one say that . . .
(for example, the sacraments of the New Law are not necessary
for salvation) let him be anathema." The very core and heart
of dogmatic work, however, is not in these anathemas, but in the
positive exposition of what Catholic faith holds on each of the
controverted points of dogma; a style and form of exposition,
which is straightforward, noble in its language, steeped in biblical
and patristic modes of expression, and persuasive in its clarity, in
its careful avoidance of the trappings of scholastic syllogism and
dialectic artifice.

This is not so by accident but by design, for the emphasis on
positive theology was part of the *reformatio ecclesiae* which in no
unmistakable words had been set forth as the all-pervading purpose of the Council. Nor was it by accident that the task of formulating the *Admonitio,* which was to set the tone, to create the
general atmosphere, as it were, for the Council's work, had been
given to Pole, to the man for whom theology was above all part
and parcel of espousing the cause of Christ in life and thought,
and not a matter of abstract speculation. He had (if I may say
this in parenthesis) to suffer for it, like other churchmen of the
time with whom he shared the fundamental belief in the need for
re-formatio; he had to suffer for it at the hands of smaller men
and narrower minds. Less than a year after the opening session,
in October, 1546, he asked the Pope to be relieved of his duties as
legate, and since it was known that he was not in all points
pleased with the final form of the decree on justification, rumor
had it that he had actually been removed as unreliable.[18] There
was at Trent the bishop of Chironissa on the island of Crete, a
Franciscan whom everybody called the Little Greek, *Grechetto,*
who was always ready to tell how he had managed to be nom-
inated to his little bishopric so he could get out of the "misery" of
life in the monastery and who also managed to live in the fair
city of Venice most of the time.[19] Grechetto used to write letters
to Cardinal Farnese, the Pope's nephew in Rome, in which he

---

[18] For Pole's resignations and the rumors connected with it, see H. Jedin,
Geschichte des Konzils von Trient II (Freiburg, 1957), 236 f. and n. 27 (p. 492).
[19] Cf. Jedin, *Geschichte* II, 69, 151, 476 n.6.

denounced other prelates of being secret sympathizers with Luther; and it is significant that his denunciations included Pole, together with Cardinal Morone, the General of the Augustinians, Seripando, and the late Cardinal Contarini; all men who were on the front lines of the battle for *reformatio ecclesiae.*

Reformatio ecclesiae—the little Greek, the notorious absentee bishop, may have had his personal reasons to dislike the very thought of it and to profess loudly that orthodoxy was all that mattered. But he was not the only one to dislike the word as well as the thing itself. Is it not strange that even today we hesitate to use the word and to speak, in connection with Trent, of reformation? Why is it that we have allowed this word to become a prerogative of the movement in the sixteenth century which was not a *reformatio* but a *deformatio,* not a "forming afresh" but a revolution? We speak, it is true, of the "Catholic Reform"; and we have abandoned, by and large, the rather odious term of "Counter-reformation" to designate all that the Council of Trent stood for; but we are afraid, are we not, to call it Reformation?

I am not trying here to indulge in linguistic or semantic niceties. But the point should be made that the Fathers of Trent had no intention of letting the Protestants get away with monopolizing the concept of *reformatio ecclesiae* and letting it become synonymous with turning upside down the very concept of the Church universal. The Fathers of Trent were fully aware that *reformatio* was a fighting word, and they courageously adopted it in its true and deeper meaning; re-forming and regenerating the people of God to become a visible likeness of the exemplary *forma* itself, the *forma* of the God-Man.[20]

We have to keep in mind, or rather to recapture, this vital concern because through various historical circumstances it has become a common attitude to take the integrated achievement of the Council of Trent apart and look at its fortification of Catholic faith as something separate from its reformatory work. From this separation there has resulted the popular image of Trent as the

---

[20] For the theology of *reformatio* in the patristic age, see G. Ladner, *The Idea of Reform* (Harvard University Press, 1959); for the era of Trent and after Trent, H. Jedin, *Katholische Reformation oder Gegen-reformation?* (Luzern, 1946).

Council which built a wall around Catholicism, a fortress within which the embattled old Faith could retire, clinging ever more stubbornly (to use a hostile word) or ever more righteously, to its old forms of worship and discipline.

Whoever takes the time to read the decress and canons of Trent, and in particular whoever reads the proceedings with all the detail recorded in the *Acta,* will soon notice that such an image is a caricature in every sense of the word. The Council was far from being a docile, unanimous flock endorsing curial and papal wishes; it was also far from restricting its attentions only to those within the fold, and from shirking its duty to lead back those that had torn themselves away.

This last named goal, as we all know, the Council did not reach. "Peace and unity of the Church," which, in the first session of December, 1545, had been determined as one of the principal aims of the Council, was not restored. A century before Luther, it had been possible to isolate and localize the revolutionary force of Bohemian Hussitism. But now, during the first half of the sixteenth century, the breakdown of the unity, of the one *Respublica Christiana,* had become an established fact. We are so accustomed today to the existence of Christian bodies outside the Catholic Church that it is difficult for us to realize what a stunning blow it meant for the men of the sixteenth century, when they became aware of this fact. It was a collapse of basic concepts that had never been questioned before. For nothing was more alien to the minds of all, Catholics, Lutherans, Calvinists, Anglicans, than the idea that there could be two or three or four Christianities. The standard bearers of the revolution no less than the champions of the old Faith were, until the mid-forties of the century, still convinced that there could be only "one Church"; and neither the vicious attacks on Rome, on the one side, nor the Catholic efforts to extirpate heretical teachings of the innovators, on the other, must blind us to the fact that in seeking *reformatio* of the Church they all had also unity in mind.

The tragedy is, *first,* that on the Protestant side *reformatio* came to mean not only eradication of corrupt abuses, but abolition of the fundamental structure of the mystical body itself. *Second,* the vacuum of spiritual authority which the new teachings had created was, almost by necessity, filled by the secular powers and that thereby it often happened that politics instead of theology were put to work to decide the fate of religion. *Third,* as a reaction to the course the religious revolution had taken, resistance against reforming life and discipline of the Church, at the papal curia, among the episcopate, and so on down, sought shelter behind the defense of faith. *Fourth,* the position of the pope as ruler of the pontifical states (and likewise the position of the German bishops as ruling princes within the framework of the Empire) enmeshed the hierarchy in political constellations on the national and the international scene, in wars, alliances, and counteralliances which made it well-nigh imposisble to treat the cause of Christ independently from worldly interests, that is, from the political problems of the balance of power.

There were many other unfortunate contingencies, but it was chiefly because of these four truly tragic factors that the Council was delayed, and delayed for more than a quarter of a century after Luther's first challenge. By the time it opened at Trent in 1545, a whole generation had grown up that was alienated from the Church; ten lears later, the peace of Augsburg between the Emperor Charles V and the Protestant Estates formally acknowledged the legitimate existence of two religions within the Empire. In those ten years, also, the Council had been twice suspended (between 1548 and 1551, and again in 1552); its decrees still awaited papal confirmation; hence, they were not yet binding.[21] Only once in all those years, during the convocation of 1551-1552 (under Julius III) did the patient efforts of the popes succeed in bringing also Protestant theologians to attend the Council, where they were expected to take their place as consultants side by side with the Catholic theologians; but no common ground was left any more for fruitful discussions. Invitations to the dissidents were repeated in 1561 and 1562, with safe-conduct and all, but they were of no avail. The work of reforming had to be done

---

[21] This point, often overlooked, is stressed in Jedin's article, "Analekten zur Reformtätigkeit der Päpste Julius' III. und Pauls IV.," *Römische Quartalschrift* 42 (1934), 316, 329.

without them; it had to be done by those and for the sake of those who would stay with the Church and in the Church.[22]

In the study of the reformatory work of the Council of Trent, two historical constructions must be rejected: (1) It is not true that in the early sixteenth century the Church was so hopelessly rooted in superstitious practices, greedy abuses, and worldly interests that it could no longer be regenerated from within but only by a revolution such as Luther's. Nor is it true that the Tridentine Reform only covered up the bad state of affairs and stifled the critics. (2) But it is equally false to point to the existence, before Luther came, of papal decrees on the abolition of abuses; to the existence of the laws adopted at the Fifth Lateran Council under Julius II and Leo X; and to the various movements of fostering a spiritual renewal that sprang up in different parts of Christendom during the fifteenth and the early sixteenth century—and to conclude that all this would have eventually led to a universal reform, had it not been disturbed and set back by the innovators.

To speculate this way is daydreaming.[23] Even the mild measures decreed by the Fifth Lateran Council remained dead letters because it was so easy it obtain dispensation in Rome from their observance. There remained enough loopholes which the laws of the Church left for those who were seeking easy appointments to remunerative bishoprics or parishes or posts in cathedral chapters and other preferments, without being bound to exercise the respective functions in person. In addition the Church had given away in many nations her control over such matters by concordats which placed these appointments in the hands of the secular rulers. Without a new inner life, in other words, without reforming the persons that were to apply and observe the laws, things had to become worse before they could become better.

This leads us to a further point which we must keep in mind. Many of the ills that beset the Church at the time, and had indeed beset it for centuries, had their roots in administrative and financial

---

[22] Cf. S. Kuttner, "Papal Efforts toward Protestant Representation at Trent," *Review of Politics,* 10 (1948), 427 ff., esp. at pp. 434-436.

[23] Cf. Jedin, *Geschichte* I (1949), 132, concluding remarks of the chapter on *Selbstreform,* pp. 93-132. For the ineffectual Lateran decrees, *ibid.* 105 f.

practices of the papal government. Laws which forbade, for example, certain malpractices in ecclesiastical appointments existed ever since the twelfth century. But what could they accomplish if the papacy flouted them by granting dispensations from such laws as a matter of routine? In other words, what good would a reformation of the canon law do if it was not a *reformatio* of the members and the head of the Church militant? But with this formula, *in capite et membris,* Christianity would have been back at the troubles of Constance and Basel, the doctrines of conciliar supremacy and constitutional restriction of the pope by the councils; of the council legislating for the pope and telling him how to run his own household and his papal office; of limiting him in the use of the plenitude of his power. This would have been the end of the divine commission given to Peter. Notwithstanding the triumph of the papacy over the last schism, perpetrated by the Council of Basel, the so-called conciliar theory was by no means dead among the faithful a century later when the Council of Trent opened. The scandals of such pontificates as those of a Sixtus IV, an Alexander VI, a Leo X, kept alive the problem how the Church can be saved from a notoriously bad pope. These scandals prompted ranking theologians and canonists time and again to investigate whether under certain extreme circumstances the papal power would not devolve to the cardinals or to the universal episcopate.[24] There is no doubt that the spectre of Basel and Constance explains why the fear of a new council overshadowed all papal policies in the long years between the first condemnation of Luther and the convocation of the Council of Trent. It also remains to the eternal credit of Paul III, himself no saint, that he dared to meet the challenge. The only way was for the Pope himself to begin reforming the papacy, the reform of the head: then the reform of the members could be placed in the council's hands.

We may say that the Catholic Reformation began with the report of the commission of cardinals (among whom were the newly appointed ardent reformers, Contarini, Pole, Carafa), the

---

[24] For examples of this line of thought, outside the group of conciliarist writers, see *ibid.* 74 ff., 21.

Consilium de emendanda ecclesia of 1537. The celebrated document[25] minced no words in saying that the will of the Supreme Pontiff must be informed by right reason; else his plenitude of power will be destructive of the common good instead of edifying the Church. The report examined, one by one, the canons which had led to the decay of the care of souls all over Christendom, and much of it was laid at the doorstep of the Curia itself. The commission recommended a number of drastic measures, many of which ran counter to the vested interests of the curial bureaucracy; no wonder that the proposals gave the signal to a long drawn struggle between progressives and conservatives at the Curia, and that the measures which were eventually decreed for curial reform by Paul III in 1546 and by Julius III in 1554 more than once bogged down, or remained behind what was desirable.[26]

In the meantime the Fathers assembled at Trent had tackled three basic problems of reform, the improvement of clerical education, the law of preaching, and the hotly debated issue of the obligation of residence for bishops and pastors. As regards the first point, no more was done in 1546 than reinforcing the old law which demanded that in each cathedral church there should be an endowed post for a master of theology—only much later, in 1563 did the Council resolve to turn away from medieval forms of instruction and to create a completely new institution, the seminary.[27] With regard to preaching, the obligation of bishops and rectors of parishes to preach the word of God on Sundays and solemn feast days was laid down and penalties for its neglect were established. Religious would need the bishop's permission to preach in churches that were not of their own order. In this matter the bishops would have disciplinary authority even over the exempt orders, an authority to be exercised in the name and on behalf of the Holy See. This form was chosen so as to preserve the nature of privileges of exemption: the bishops would have the right of supervision in this matter not by virtue of their

---

[25] CT 12, ed. V. Schweitzer (Freiburg, 1930), 131-145, with bibliography.

[26] Documents of reform under Paul III are collected by Ehses in CT 4.449-512; under Julius III, by Schweitzer and Jedin in CT 13 (1938), 165-315; cf. also Jedin, *Analekten* (n.21), pp. 311 ff.

[27] *Sess. 5, de ref.* c.1; *sess. 23, de ref.* c.18.

own episcopal jurisdiction but as permanent delegates of the authority which had granted the exemption, the Apostolic See.[28]

The very core of the problems of reform, however, was reached when discussions began on the obligation of residence. It is difficult for the modern mind to grasp the immense importance this point had in the history of the Council and the embittered fighting it caused during the first convocation and, with even greater passion, during the third convocation.

We have to recall here the medieval conception in which bishoprics, parochial churches, chaplaincies, and other institutions destined to the care of souls were considered not simply as offices with appropriate remuneration for the incumbent. Since the income was derived from endowment, the capital value and its revenue, which had the technical name of *beneficium*, came to be considered as an entity in itself which could be separated from the duties inherent to the office. Thus, in the case of a bishopric, the bishop might ask for and receive a dispensation from exercising in person his duties of ruling the flock entrusted to him, of ordaining the clergy, of confirming, of consecrating holy oils and churches. With this dispensation he could then live elsewhere— in Rome, in Venice, at the court of a secular sovereign—leaving the care of the diocese to vicars and auxiliaries. But all the time he would go on enjoying the income from the endowment of the episcopal see, with no other obligation than paying some modest stipend out of this income to those who did the actual labor in the Lord's vineyard. The same was possible on the parochial level: the revenue, the parish benefice, might be in the hand of an absentee, or of a corporate body (monasteries, universities, cathedral chapters) which would have the parish work done by a vicar.

In ths way, the absentee bishop or absentee pastor might even cumulate the revenue of several benefices. The medieval law had time and again issued prohibitions against such cumulation, at least of incompatible benefices, that is, the cumulation of revenues from several offices if these offices carried the obligation of care of souls. But there was again the loophole of dispensations that could be obtained from Rome. In order to provide a living for

---

[28] *Sess.* 5, *de ref.* c.2.

the ever-growing personnel of the papal administrations, in the first line for the cardinals, laxity in granting such dispensations for the so-called pluralists was a most convenient practical solution.

The popes of the Renaissance had set the example of raising their relatives—even lads of twelve or sixteen—to the cardinalate, conferring upon them at the same time one or several bishoprics, not counting other benefices. A cardinal also might renounce such a bishopric in favor of a relative, retaining, however, part of the income and the right that the title should revert to him if the relative resigned in turn *(regressus)*. He might hold the revenue of abbeys as titular *(in commendam)* and pay the actual abbot and the community a stipend out it. He could burden the benefice or benefices he owned or resigned with pensions in favor of his household, his secretaries, and assistants. Cardinal Ippolito d'Este in 1519 resigned the metropolitan see of Milan (with an income of 3,000 florins) in favor of his nephew, then eleven years old, while retaining the archbishopric of Capua (2,000 fl.) and the episcopal sees of Ferrara, his native city (4,000 fl.), and the wealthy Eger in faraway Hungary (10,000 fl.).[29] The new archbishop of Milan was eventually consecrated in 1536; in thirty years from 1520 to 1550, when he resigned the see, he never set foot in his cathedral.[30]

What happened at the papal court happened elsewhere. Absentee bishops were ministers of state, ambassadors, educators of princes, etc.; in short, throughout Christendom innumerable churches were orphaned, their actual administration in the hands of hirelings.

The Council passed, in 1547, the first two decrees making residence in their sees mandatory for bishops (and correspondingly for rectors of parishes). It regulated the appointment to parochial and other offices, and laid down the obligation of those appointed

---

[29] See von Gulik-Eubel, *Hierarchia catholica medii aevi* III (Münster, 1910), 257 (s.v. *Mediolanen.*), and the entries under the other sees in Eubel, *op. cit.* II (2nd ed., 1914) and III. Cf. Jedin, "*Il significato del Concilio di Trento nella storia della Chiesa,*" *Gregorianum* 26 (1945), 129; other examples of pluralists, e.g., in Philip Hughes, *History of the Church*, III (London, 1947), 535-538.

[30] *Hier. cath.,* III, 257, n.3 s.v. *Mediolanen.*

to obtain the requisite ordination within reasonable time; it restricted the privilege, until then easily obtainable for a cleric, to receive ordination from any bishop he chose, because this fantastic abuse made every control of the ordinary over the worthiness of the candidate impossible.[31] But while these decrees undoubtedly marked a progress in the combating of pluralism and laxity, they were not sufficient. They were not strict enough in closing all the loopholes; and since papal confirmation of the decrees was not yet forthcoming, they remained largely unobserved. Let me cite two significant facts. As late as 1556 Cardinal Alessandro Farnese, the nephew of Paul III, drew up the following inventory of his vested rights: a pension from the episcopal See of Avignon (which he had resigned), rights of reversion for ten bishoprics, twenty-six abbeys, and more than a hundred lesser benefices.[32] The other fact is that in 1563 the Council found it necessary to revise the decree on residence of 1547 because its terms had been misconstrued by many. According to the earlier decree, bishops absent from their see for six consecutive months were to forfeit one-fourth of the revenue. This, we read in Session XXIII, had been taken by many as a permission to stay away without excuse for any period under six months![33]

It was, indeed, only during the last convocation that more efficient reform decrees (of which that on residence is only one example) were enacted. The ordinaries, for example, were empowered to examine any dispensations obtained from the curia by their diocesans, so as to establish whether they had been granted on a truthful petition.[34] In short, only during the last period of the Council do we find, to use a colloquial term, a legislation with teeth in it. That this was possible was premised on two important alterations. A change of heart had taken place in Rome itself, by permitting the Council to legislate in a manner that would protect the integrity of diocesan life *also* against curial routine. A change of heart had come within the episcopate, where we can observe

---

[31] *Sess.* 6, *de ref.* cc.1-5; *sess.* 7, *de ref.* cc.1-6, 13.

[32] CT 13.320, n.4; cf. Jedin, *Analekten*, p. 317 n.13.

[33] *Sess.* 23, *de ref.* c.1: ". . . as if on the strength of that decree it were lawful to be absent for five continuous months."

[34] *Sess.* 22, *de ref.* c.5.

the emergence of a new type of shepherd: the bishop for whom indeed the salvation of souls was the overriding concern—*salus animarum suprema lex*—the type of bishop which had been represented by hardly a handful of saintly men twenty years before,[35] but which was by now no longer the exception.

The decrees of 1563 are largely the work of Cardinal Morone, one of the few men we have to single out when we want to remember those to whom the *reformatio ecclesiae* owes most. His work covers from the early years of preparing the Council when he, only twenty-eight years of age, was Paul III's nuncio at the Court of Vienna, to his masterful handling of the Council's great crisis in 1562, the year before it came to its end.[36] The immediate cause of the crisis had been, once more, the problem of residence. The French and the Spanish bishops wanted this to be carried from the disciplinary field into the sphere of dogma. They contended the Council should define that the obligation of the bishop to reside in his see is an obligation of divine law, with the consequence that thereby not even the Pope could grant a dispensation from it.

The battle for the definition of the divine law of residence was not, as has sometimes been said, a mere strategic trick to bolster episcopal independence from the primatial power of the Pope. Those who fought for this definition could claim for it the theological authority of the great Cajetan.[37] Yet, in the practical conflict of interests and mutual animosities, it could become a weapon of politics, of politics with a vengeance, by uniting in each country the episcopate with the secular ruler in a common cause, that of limiting papal power. It brought ammunition to the curialists, the group of *zelanti* headed by Cardinal Simonetta, who labored for eliminating legislation on residence altogether from the agenda. No sessions were held for ten months, from

---

[35] For a very illuminating history of one section of the episcopate in this period, see G. Alberigo, *I vescovi italiani al Concilio di Trento (1545-1547)* (Florence, 1959).

[36] H. Jedin, *Krisis und Wendepunkt des Konzils von Trient 1562-63* (Würzburg, 1941).

[37] In his commentary on the *Summa theologica* of St. Thomas, 2.2, q.185, art.5, written in 1517. Cf. Alberigo, *op. cit.* pp. 410 ff.

September, 1562, while the wranglings and diplomatic maneuverings went on behind the scenes. Finally, in April, 1563, Morone came to Trent as the new presiding legate, and all his ability was needed to bring about the compromise by which a strong decree on residence was enacted in July. The question of the *ius divinum* was passed over in silence.[38] The time for defining the relation between the two God-given powers in the Church, papacy and episcopacy, was not ripe (it might be at hand in our day), but we have to be eternally grateful to the Council of Trent for having restored, by a practical, disciplinary solution the normal care of souls. Gratitude is due also for having created a basis on which the spiritual life of Christ's flock could take new strength. It remained to be seen what the papacy and the episcopate, the clergy to be formed in the new seminaries, and the Catholic people would make of this blueprint of spiritual regeneration. But that is another chapter in the history of the Church.

Stephan Kuttner

---

[38] *Sess.* 25, *de ref.* c.1; cf. *sess.* 24 *de ref.* c.12.

The Church Faces The Modern World:
The Vatican Council, 1869-1870

The Church Faces the Modern World:
The Vatican Council, 1869-1870

IT WOULD BE RASH, indeed, to attempt to do justice to the manifold aspects of the Vatican Council within the limits of this chapter. For our purpose it will be sufficient at the outset merely to recall the following facts. It was the first ecumenical gathering in over 300 years; it was more than five years in preparation; it drew nearly 750 bishops from every corner of the globe; its sessions lasted over nine months; the official record of its proceedings fill five large volumes in the continuation of Mansi's famous conciliar collections;[1] and the Council has been universally regarded as having marked, both in doctrine and in the Church's relationship to the State, a significant and enduring milestone in modern ecclesiastical history. Even a momentary reflection on these purely external features makes it evident why limitation is a stern necessity.

In a certain sense the Vatican Council set its own limitations, for it was the only one of the twenty ecumenical assemblies to date that enacted no disciplinary decrees. True, there was extended discussion of disciplinary matters during the bishops' time in Rome, but their debates ended in no formal legislation on this head, as was the case, for example, with the dogmatic constitutions which by mid-summer of 1870 had emerged in the *Dei Filius* on Catholic faith and the *Pastor Aeternus*[2] on the primacy and infallibility of the Pope. A second limiting factor came from with-

---

[1] Mansi, *Collectio Conciliorum* . . . Volumes XLIX-LIII (Paris, 1923-1927).

[2] The apostolic constitutions, *Dei Filius* of April 24, 1870, and *Pastor Aeternus* of July 18, 1870, are contained in Latin and English texts on facing pages in an appendix to Cuthbert Butler, O.S.B., *The Vatican Council* (London, 1930), II, 247-295.

out. On July 19, the day after the final vote on infallibility, France declared war on Prussia, and in the face of this grave danger most of the bishops quickly departed for home. Sessions continued to be held through August and September, but the effort to reassemble the bishops at Malines in Belgium, or elsewhere, failed, and on October 20 Pius IX prorogued the Council, a status that technically obtained for the succeeding ninety years, until Pope John XXIII's action in summoning a new council to bear the name of Vatican Council II may be said to have written an end to the 1870 gathering.

I shall, then, confine myself to four main points. First, in the hope of conveying an impression of the intellectual climate in which the assembly met and carried out its work, I shall try to sketch, in a few broad strokes, the general *mise en scène* of these years of the mid-century. Second, certain features of the Council's preparatory stages will be presented from the viewpoint of three highly interested groups: 1) the theologians, gathered in Rome at an early date to shape and refine the material for the conciliar agenda; 2) the bishops, as yet at home in their dioceses, reflecting Catholic reaction at a distance from the Eternal City; 3) the statesmen, representative of how the Council appeared either to those outside the Church, or to Catholics prominent in the service of the State. Thus with the scene having been laid, the theologians having completed their task, with the bishops gradually converging on Rome by the early winter of 1869, and with the secular governments watching suspiciously from afar, we shall, I hope, be in a position to treat the third major point. And here lack of space will compel me to forego any treatment of the theologically important debates that led to the constitution on Catholic faith, as well as any further mention of the lively exchange of views on disciplinary matters; in other words, in point three we shall proceed directly to the most controverted question, the definition of papal infallibility. Finally, with the bishops' decisive vote on that crucial issue having been taken on July 18, and the outbreak of the Franco-Prussian War twenty-four hours thereafter, which for all practical purposes brought the Council to an end, an attempt will be made to interpret its significance in terms once more of three groups: 1) the Roman Curia or the central governing body of the Holy See; 2) the universal Church as represented by the bishops and priests; 3) the secular interests as heard through the cabinet ministers, diplomats, and parliamentarians of an age that prided itself on its scientific advance and on its success in having discovered what it believed to be the avenue to unlimited human progress.

In one respect the reaction of the mid-nineteenth century toward the Catholic Church resembled that of most generations that had preceded it. Few men of commanding station and influence had indulged themselves in the luxury of indifference toward the ebb and flow of Catholic life, regardless of the casualness with which they may have seemed to view it. And in this the ranking figures of the 1860's were no exception. Ecclesiastical developments were closely observed with the eye of either friend or foe, and the strength of these two opposing schools of thought *vis-à-vis* the papacy would be felt from Pio Nono's earliest intimation that it was his intention to issue the historic summons.

First, let me quickly review what might be called the friendly factors conducing to the convening of a council. Here a prominent place should be assigned to the personality of the reigning pontiff. Warmhearted, impetuous, free of official hauteur, and easily approachable, Pius IX had endeared himself to great numbers of people since the opening of his reign in 1846. True, in later years he had lost heavily with men of liberal sympathies; yet Frédéric Ozanam's description of him in the early months of the pontificate retained sufficient validity two decades later to warrant being heard. In January, 1847, Ozanam wrote to a friend from Rome:

> This pontiff whom one encounters on foot in the streets, who this week went one evening to visit a poor widow and to aid her without making himself known, who preaches each fortnight to the people assembled at San Andrea della Valle, this courageous reformer of abuse in the temporal government, seems truly sent by God to conclude the great affair of the nineteenth century, the alliance of religion and of liberty.[3]

---

[3] Frédéric Ozanam to Prosper Guéranger, Rome, January 29, 1847, quoted in Roger Aubert, *Le Pontificat de Pie IX, 1846-1878* (Paris, 1952), p. 20.

Although it proved to be a sadly mistaken prophecy, the pontiff, nonetheless, held the affection of many to the end, and no small part of the attraction he had for others were his *bons mots* that went the round of certain circles the world over. Some weeks after the opening of the Council, for example, in the midst of discussion on the advisability of introducing the controverted question of the pope's infallibility, Pius IX was quoted in one of his frequent plays on words when he remarked, *"Non so se il Papa uscirà di questo Concilio fallibile od infallibile; ma questo è certo che sarà fallito."*[4]

Of deeper significance, however, than the personality of any single churchman was the rising tide of a new ultramontanist movement that had been gaining ground since the opening of the century, and that served to create an enthusiasm for the papacy in sharp contrast to the cold and aloof manner in which even many Catholics had regarded the See of Peter through most of the eighteenth century. In German-speaking lands one sensed its dawning manifestation with the succession of prominent converts to Catholicism which began with Friedrich Leopold Count von Stolberg in 1800 and which continued with the Schlegels and their literary associates, as well as the return to an ardent practice of the Faith after years of estrangement of men like Josef Görres and Clemens Brentano. *Der Katholik* of Mainz and the *Stimmen aus Maria Laach* of the German Jesuits gave the conservatives a voice, while the *Kölnische Blatter* after 1860 furnished the same to the German Catholics of liberal sympathies. A decided impetus had been provided in November, 1837, by the blunder of the Prussian government in arresting and imprisoning the Archbishops of Cologne and Gnesen-Posen in a dispute about jurisdiction over mixed marriages. The release of the two archbishops in 1840 by the new King Frederick William IV amounted to an admission of defeat on the part of the State, and the consequent victory for the Church had a bracing effect on Catholics of all shades of opinion.

Meanwhile, the publication in 1802 of Chateaubriand's *Génie du Christianisme* foreshadowed a reviving religious trend in

---

[4] Butler, *op. cit.*, I, 170, n. 1.

France, and seventeen years later neo-ultramontanism received a classic expression in *Du Pape,* the celebrated work of Comte Joseph de Maistre, the tone of which blended well with many of the dominant ideas of the romantic movement then in its heyday. It was France, too, that was the scene, in the generation that preceded the Council, of the series of apparitions of the Virgin, first to Catherine Labouré in 1831 and then at La Salette, a phenomenon which was crowned, as it were, in 1854 by Pius IX's definition of Mary's immaculate conception, so soon to be confirmed by our Lady herself when in March, 1858, at Lourdes she answered Bernadette Soubirous' question concerning her identity. It was in France, likewise, that there was founded in 1822, through the inspiration of Pauline Jaricot and her associates, the Society for the Propagation of the Faith, that was destined not only to play a significant role in the spread of the Faith in pagan lands but to rekindle it in the hearts of many for whom it had all but disappeared. Here, as well, were witnessed the mounting pilgrimages to the saintly cure at Ars, at times so numerous as almost to suggest a mass movement. Running parallel, therefore, to the scientific and secularist spirit of French public life was this extraordinary revival in the nation's ancient faith. For if at this time France gave birth to the father of positivism in Comte, and to the parent of anarchism in Proudhon, it was simultaneously the home of Ozanam and his strikingly successful Society of St. Vincent de Paul, of a highly articulate group of liberal Catholics who in 1843 revived *Le Correspondant* in the form of a monthly journal, as well as of Louis Veuillot whose enthusiasm for the See of Peter knew no bounds and whose newspaper, *l'Univers,* became the stoutest ultramontanist organ to be read outside Rome.

The most original and challenging aspects of mid-century Catholicism arose, therefore, in Germany and France. Yet it would be a mistake to ignore the Oxford Movement, which by 1840 had become identified as the *causa agitans* for the surprising number of distinguished English minds that made their submission to Rome during that decade. Among these men, none was more articulate than William George Ward, who took over the *Dublin Review* in 1863 and soon made it the most pronounced ultramontanist journal in the English-speaking world. And Ward's editorship opened at the very time that the *Home and Foreign Review* of Sir John Acton and Richard Simpson, another convert, bowed to ecclesiastical authority and ceased publication, thus leaving the English Catholics of liberal sympathies with no outlet for their views. Likewise among traditionally Catholic peoples like the Belgians, Poles, and Irish, the old Faith took on new meaning in these years as a support to the strong nationalist spirit that prompted them to rise against their Protestant and Orthodox overlords. Needless to say, most of this religious ferment north of the Alps was a source of joy—and of hope—to Rome, gravely threatened as it now was by the full tide of the *Risorgimento.* Yet Rome was not without its own resources, for at this time Italian ultramontanism had its most effective organ in the Eternal City in the bi-weekly journal of the Jesuits, the *Civiltà Cattolica,* which was rounding out the first decade of its existence.

These were the factors, then, that were conducive to the holding of a general council. But it was not the Catholics, whether of the liberal or ultramontanist persuasion, who set the prevailing patterns of thought for western Europe at the mid-century. And that brings us to the forces militating against the Council's success. Among these were the rationalism and religious indifference that pervaded so large a part of the upper classes, for among them the toll taken by the philosophy of the Enlightenment had been exceedingly heavy. In fact, the Catholic revival of the years after 1800 had touched hardly more than a fraction of those in high places. Even more serious, perhaps, was the widespread religious illiteracy among the masses. The French Revolution and its aftermath had thinned the ranks of the clergy, and those who later pursued a religious vocation to completion experienced in their seminary training a lack of solid preparation and of intellectual stimulation that left them quite unfit to cope with the problems of their time. The intellectual and scientific elite, of course, were in good measure hostile to traditional religion, and at centers like Tübingen with its higher criticism of the Scriptures, and Berlin with its school of scientific history, of which Leopold von Ranke was the soul, the imagination of the learned world's future leaders was often captured and permanently alienated from religious values. What was equally unfortunate was the absence of a corresponding intellectual force and an atmosphere of freedom of inquiry in Catholic circles to offset the damage to souls and to win them back to the Church. When it is recalled that as late as 1820 a book that maintained that the earth went around the sun was refused the ecclesiastical *imprimatur* at Rome, although ᵒr two centuries had passed since Copernicus' famous treatise won general acceptance, it is not difficult to understand wh achievements of solitary Catholic scientists like Gregor ᵀ n Mendel and Louis Pasteur should have had relatively little ᵖct in offsetting attacks by secular scientists and philosophicaᶫ rals upon the Catholic Church as the enemy of learning.

Obviously, natural science was not the proper domain of churchmen who might, therefore, be excused for having done so little to promote it, even though they could scarcely be excused for refusing to accept its clearly demonstrated facts. Theology and philosophy were their domain, yet here Catholic achievement in the generation immediately preceding the Council was anything but distinguished. The Catholic University of Louvain, reopened in 1834 after an interval of forty years, was for much of this time absorbed in the ontologist controversy centering around Professor Casimir Ubaghs whose teaching was censured by the Holy See in 1864. At Rome itself the higher schools of philosophy and theology, in which one might have anticipated a serious concern with the moral aspects of contemporary problems, were still intellectually stagnant, a condition that endured into the next pontificate until they were finally stirred by the Thomistic revival initiated by Pope Leo XIII. For example, a priest-historian of exemplary piety like Johannes Janssen was shocked on a visit to Rome in 1864 in seeing the neglect in exploiting the Eternal City's incomparable research resources.[5] In Germany alone could one

---

[5] Janssen to Maria von Sydow, Rome, March 13, 1864, Ludwig Freiherr von Pastor (Ed.) *Johannes Janssens Briefe* (Freiburg im B., 1920), I, 285. A similar impression was created in the mind of Newman when he went to Rome to finish his studies for the priesthood in 1846. Not long after his arrival he told John D. Dalgairns, "Hope [James R. Hope-Scott] told me we should find very little theol-

then find in any numbers Catholic scholars who were a match for their secular counterparts. But even the celebrated Munich school could make little impression on a generation captivated after 1859 by Darwin's *Origin of Species* and by the more damaging *La Vie de Jésus* of Ernest Renan that appeared four years later, to mention only two works that enjoyed an immense vogue and that destroyed the belief of so many erstwhile Christians in the authenticity of the Scriptures and the divinity of Christ. Had the Church been able to marshal an array of first-class scholars, such as the French Benedictines of St. Maur and the Jesuit Bollandists of the Low Countries who had served Catholic scholarship so admirably in the seventeenth century, much of the damage might have been repaired. Instead, the energies of too many writers who caught the fancy of the masses, and by the same token repelled the learned, were directed largely toward the production of popular and uncritical works that provided no defense of the Catholic position where it was under the heaviest fire. Wilfrid Ward described the situation in these words:

> Incredible and unsupported stories in history and extravagances in dogma were the order of the day. . . . The disparagement of the individual intellect, which Bonald had so carefully limited, was extended by later writers, without his genius, to the disparagement of scientific research itself; and even after the condemnation by Rome of such exaggerations, the temper which prompted them—of distrust of modern science and civilisation—remained.[6]

Equally formidable were the forces ranged against revealed religion in the marketplace and in government. To most men who accorded it any heed at all the *Communist Manifesto* of Marx and Engels in 1848 was but a bizarre pamphlet by two obscure German radicals. But by 1864 the force that lay behind that publication had gathered enough momentum for Marx to organize the

ogy here, and a talk we had yesterday with one of the Jesuit fathers here shows we shall find little philosophy." Newman to Dalgairns, Rome, November 22, 1846, Wilfrid Ward, *The Life of John Henry Cardinal Newman* (London, 1912), I, 167. Cf. also his later letters to Dalgairns (*Ibid.*, I, 169, 172-173). Hereafter this work will be cited as: Ward, *Newman*.

[6] Wilfrid Ward, *William George Ward and the Catholic Revival* (London, 1893), p. 120.

First International and to earn a condemnation in Pius IX's encyclical *Quanta cura,* published on December 8 of that year. In the economic and social order a powerful attack had thus been mounted upon all the traditional values which showed every sign of spreading. In government the moral power that the popes had once wielded had long since disappeared, and the episode of Ercole Cardinal Consalvi, Pius VII's Secretary of State, at the Congress of Vienna in 1814-1815, was only the exception that proved the rule of a virtual exclusion of papal influence from international affairs. Observers of the political order were afforded a rehearsal, as it were, for Otto von Bismarck's era of *Realpolitik* by Prussia's two brief wars, first against Denmark (1864) and then against Austria (1866), thus giving a quick foretaste of what was in store for Europe by way of the Prussian minister-president's declared policy of "blood and iron." And if Great Britain was not so nakedly provocative as Prussia, there was little by way of religious persuasion informing its official policies, and certainly no Catholic influence, as the national hysteria against the so-called "papal aggression" demonstrated when Pio Nono restored the hierarchy to England in 1850.

Nor was the public temper toward the Church more friendly across the Atlantic where three years later the Know-Nothing agitation in the United States created a series of riots in major American cities on the occasion of the visit of Pius IX's representative, Archbishop Gaetano Bedini. One would not be warranted in dismissing the Know-Nothing excesses as solely the doing of an ignorant rabble, and, therefore, in no sense typical of national sentiment, for one of the best educated Americans of that generation, George Bancroft, United States Minister to Prussia, was found a year and a half before the Council characterizing for a friend the Catholic trends in Europe in these words: "In theology the most marked phenomenon in Europe is the concentrated unity and activity of the Roman clerical party."[7] If that could be believed in the green wood, what of the dry? True, during this period there were other states that were governed by Catholic

---

[7] Bancroft to Samuel Osgood, Berlin, February 21, 1868, M.A. DeWolfe Howe, *The Life and Letters of George Bancroft* (New York, 1908), II, 203.

rulers who in some instances regulated their ecclesiastical affairs by concordats with the Holy See, but in no instance was there any real sympathy and support for the objectives that Pius IX had in mind in summoning a general council.

Finally, and this was obviously not a professedly hostile element, there was the attitude of the Pope and the Roman Curia toward the political realities of their time. The failure of the pontiffs from Pius VI to Pius IX to comprehend, much less to accept, the fact that the day of the absolute monarchs was over, that the era of parliamentary rule had come to stay, and that such was the type of government that was winning more and more of their spiritual subjects throughout the western world—this was a barrier that tended to separate the popes, not only from their contemporaries outside the Church but even from many Catholics. Having experienced harsh, at times brutal, treatment at the hands of men who, ironically enough, liked to style themselves disciples of the liberal creed, it was altogether understandable that the pontiffs should have fought to prevent what they regarded as an evil revolutionary inheritance from taking lodgement in their own domain. But where Rome's lack of political realism unwittingly inflicted injury on the Catholic name was its refusal to distinguish between the principles of philosophical liberalism which in many respects were, indeed, totally unacceptable to Catholics, and the perfectly legitimate aspirations with which many of the Holy See's spiritual subjects supported freedom of conscience, of assembly, of speech, and of the press. In that connection if only the Roman curial officials had been able to sense the worth and wisdom in warnings from so friendly a source as that of the devout Catholic laymen who edited *Le Correspondant,* much harm might have been undone. Two months before the Council opened, the Paris journal published a notable article in which the liberal-minded editors made an eloquent and touching appeal for the reconciliation of the Church with those aspects of modern society which were above suspicion. The day of the absolute monarchy, they said, was gone, and the regime of liberty that had succeeded it was both the providential law of the new age and the test to which it now pleased God to put the world and the Church. To these laymen liberty was the supreme test of both institutions and of character, and applying the point to the Church they said:

> The Church is passing through it today. She has experienced others like it and each century brings its own. There was first of all the terrible test of persecution; then the test of schism full of turmoil and anguish; then the enervating and corrupting test of prosperity; and there is today the virile and militant test of liberty.[8]

But voices like those of *Le Correspondant* were not heeded at Rome, if they were heard, and as a consequence there was created an abyss between the mid-century papacy and the contemporary world which entailed a blurring, as it were, of the spiritual and temporal roles of the Pope, and which a generation before even Giuseppe Cardinal Sala, a member of the Roman Curia, who has been described by a recent historian as "the most clear-sighted political thinker in the Sacred College," had not thought proper to try to rectify.[9] And once strong hands like those of Consalvi and Sala had been removed from the helm both the government of the Papal States and the prestige of the pontiffs steadily deteriorated. In the eyes of most observers the nadir was reached in Gregory XVI's fiery condemnations of the universal desire for freedom, and that not excepting the Catholic Poles who in their uprising of 1830 against the oppression of Czar Nicholas I had hoped for at least the Holy Father's sympathetic understanding. By 1850 Pius IX had fallen in with many of Gregory's policies, and it was thus understandable that some statesmen and diplomats should have reacted to his call for a council as having sounded an ominous note for the political order, and that at one point the great assembly's freedom should have momentarily seemed threatened in a way that was reminiscent of the Emperor Charles V at Trent over 300 years before.

---

[8] P. Douhaire pour le Conseil de redaction, "Le Concile," *Le Correspondant* LXXX (October 10, 1869), 40.

[9] E.E.Y. Hales, *Revolution and Papacy, 1769-1846* (Garden City, New York, 1960), p. 257. The last two chapters of this work (pp. 261-295) give an excellent summary of the papacy *vis-à-vis* the political world from the restoration in 1815 to the loss of the temporal sovereignty in 1870.

Let that suffice for a description of the kind of world in which the Vatican Council was held; and let us now proceed to the preparatory stages of the gathering. It was on December 6, 1864, two days before his encyclical *Quanta cura,* with its accompanying *Syllabus of Errors,* was published, that Pio Nono first privately intimated to the cardinals of the Congregation of Rites what he had in mind. He stated that he had been thinking of a general council for a long time, and he now wished to have the cardinals' reactions to the idea. Of the twenty-one replies all but eight were favorable.[10] There then followed in the spring of 1865 a confidential letter from Pius IX to thirty-four bishops of the Latin Church and to certain Oriental prelates asking for their opinions. Again a large majority pronounced in favor with a half dozen or more raising serious doubts and objections, and it is interesting to note that among the answers eight specifically stated that they thought the pope's infallibility should be defined. Having thus satisfied himself about the support of the episcopate, the pontiff chose to make the public announcement on June 26, 1867, to a gathering of approximately 500 bishops from all over the world who had come for the celebration of the eighteenth centennial of the martyrdom of SS. Peter and Paul. A congratulatory address to Pius IX was drawn up in the name of the assembled bishops in which the convening of a council was strongly favored, although this early the voice of the minority was heard when Jacques-Marie Ginoulhiac, Bishop of Grenoble, exclaimed in a fury to William Ullathorne of Birmingham against the tactics of the Archbishop of Westminster: *"Ce n'est pas le temps de casser les vitraux."*[11]

The issue having thus been determined formally, the preparations that had been shaping for two and a half years went forward under the auspices of the directing commission of eight cardinals who, in turn, gradually evolved five major commissions to deal with Council's business under the following headings: faith and dogma; ecclesiastical discipline; religious orders; Oriental churches and foreign missions; and, finally, politico-

---

[10] The best history of the Council in English is that of Butler where an ample account of the preliminary stages may be read (I, 3-153).

[11] Butler, *op. cit.,* I, 86.

religious questions involving the relations of Church and State. The hierarchies of the principal countries were invited to send representative theologians to Rome to work on the agenda, and by November, 1868, these men had arrived and had been assigned to their respective duties. The Christmas issue of the *Civiltà Cattolica* listed their names to the total of ninety-seven, including the eight cardinals of the directing commission, and of this number about sixty were Italians, with the others drawn from various national groups.[12] John Henry Newman had received a personal invitation from both Pius IX and Félix Dupanloup, Bishop of Orléans, but the great Oratorian asked to be excused, explaining to a friend:

> I am more happy as I am, than in any other way, I can't bear the kind of trouble which I should have, if I were brought forward in any public way. Recollect, I could not be *in* the Council, unless I were a Bishop—and really and truly I am *not* a theologian. . . . Like St. Gregory Nazianzen, I like going on my own way, and having my time my own, living without pomp or state, or pressing engagements. Put me into official garb, and I am worth nothing; leave me to my-self, and every now and then I shall do something.[13]

As for the United States, the choice fell upon the outstanding American theologian of the day, James A. Corcoran, a priest of the Diocese of Charleston who had already made a name for himself at the Baltimore plenary council in October, 1866, for his knowledge of theology and canon law as well as for his use of Latin.[14] Corcoran's letters to Martin J. Spalding, Archbishop of Baltimore, afford valuable insights into some of the problems before the theologians then assembled at the Holy See. For example, early in March of 1869 he expressed dissatisfaction with the *segreto pontificio* under which they were expected to operate.

---

[12] Serie VII, V (December 26, 1868), 98-104.

[13] Newman to Sister Maria Pia Giberne, February 10, 1869, in Ward, *op. cit.*, II, 281. In the end Dr. William Weathers, President of St. Edmund's College, Ware, represented the English hierarchy.

[14] For Corcoran cf. the unpublished doctoral dissertation of Sister Mary Marcian Lowman, O.S.U., "James Andrew Corcoran: Editor, Theologian, Scholar, 1820-1889," Saint Louis University (1958).

Since the theologians were supposed to represent their bishops, Corcoran could not see how this could be done unless they consulted them from time to time and acquainted them with what was going on. "I have decided for myself," he told Spalding, "and as I would not scruple to tell you my mind and my present situation, were I in your company, I shall not hesitate to tell it by letter." At this particular time, however, he had something more serious on his mind than methods of procedure; it was the subject matter of the proposed decrees and the spirit in which it was being approached that gave him cause for misgiving. "If it were left to these theologians," he said, "the nineteenth [sic] ecumenical council would issue more decrees, I mean *doctrinal definitions,* than all its predecessors from Nice [sic] to Trent." Adding to his discomfort were the twenty some canons already approved that touched on the Church's relations to the State, in some of which, he remarked, "I verily believe the fundamental principles of our (American & common sense) political doctrine are condemned. . . ." In spite of the fact that he had stood alone, he had held out against certain decrees on which he felt the Church had no right to pronounce. As for papal infallibility, Corcoran told the archbishop nine months before the opening of the Council, "if I can judge aright, this definition is a foregone conclusion. . . ." Not unnaturally he wished to know Spalding's mind and would be glad, as he put it, "to have your sentiments on this point for my instruction and guidance."[15]

In Archbishop Spalding's reply the United States bishops' attitude was summarized on several leading questions in about as satisfactory a way as one is likely to find anywhere. Spalding was grateful for Corcoran's clear expression of views and stated that in general he endorsed them and approved his course; moreover, he was confident that all the bishops "of this region," as he expressed it, would unite in these opinions. As for the three key points of papal infallibility, the proposal to define the condemnations of the *Syllabus of Errors,* and relations of Church and State, the titular head of the American hierarchy answered as follows:

[15] Archives of the Archdiocese of Baltimore, 33-M-12, Corcoran to Spalding, Rome, March 1, 1869. Hereafter these archives will be designated as AAB.

1. We believe firmly the infallibility of the Pope ex Cathedra, but incline to think its formal definition unnecessary and perhaps inexpedient, not only for the reasons you allege, but also on account of the difficulty of fixing the precise limits of these doctrinal decisions. When they are formal—as is that of Im. Conception—there is no difficulty; but are all the declarations of Encyclicals, Allocutions, etc. to be received as doctrinal definitions? And what about the decisions of Congregations, confirmed by the Pontiff?

2. While we adhere ex corde to the principles enunciated in the Syllabus, we look upon them in *concreto* et in *subjecta materia,* not generalizing what is special, & not stretching their meanings beyond that inferrible from the circumstances to which they were applied. While freedom of worship is condemned when it implies a right not given by Christ, & is concerned . . . with introducing false worship into a Catholic country, it is not only not censurable but commendable & the only thing practicable in countries like ours, England, Russia, etc. And so of the liberty of the press, & progress in the American & Anglo-Saxon sense—not in the Liberal European. There is a wide distinction & any attempt to confound things so wide apart would be wrong & nugatory, putting us in a false position, in fact, untenable.

3. So, in regard to Church & State. The principle is all right; but the application to circumstances must vary with them. With us, & in half of Christendom, wholly impracticable; in countries once Catholic —as [France?] Austria, Spain, Italy, the tendency is to separation. It is an open question whether the Church does not lose more than she gains by the union; & it is not in the order of Providence that we are to come back to the type of primitive ages.[16]

More light could be derived from this exchange of letters if space permitted, especially in the revealing vignettes of some of

---

[16] AAB, Letterbook of Archbishop Spalding, Spalding to Corcoran, Baltimore, March 27, 1869, p. 585. Spalding further developed his thought on these subjects in a letter of June 19, 1869, to Paul Cardinal Cullen, Archbishop of Dublin, when he said: "I fear, from what little I can learn on the subject, that there will be a tendency to take very high church grounds in the approaching Council in regard not only to the infallibility of the Pope & the Syllabus in its *letter,* but also as to Union of Church & State, religious toleration, the brachium saeculare etc., etc. This last particularly would be unfortunate. We who live in a totally different state of things which is likely to be permanent & to be more & more extended, will be compelled to take a decided stand on the subject, especially the application in detail." (*Ibid.,* p. 776). If an unsigned article in the *Catholic World* of June, 1869, entitled "The Approaching Council of the Vatican" [IX, 356-366] was any indication of the state of American Catholic opinion, it was quite ill-informed and given to unwarranted expectations and predictions.

the Council's leading figures. For example, Corcoran came to know well Aloisio Cardinal Bilio, president of the dogmatic commission on which the American served, and he had the highest praise for Bilio's intelligence, kindliness, and candor. "But like too many of the rest," he said, "he has never looked boldly in the face the world in which we live and to which we are coming. The Syllabus is in his head and heart; it must be defined, every word and syllable of it."[17]

For nine months preceding the opening of the Council, strenuous attempts were made by the so-called majority and minority parties among the bishops to persuade the uncommitted on the validity of their respective positions on a number of questions, but especially on the definition of papal infallibility. In a sense the strife that followed was inevitable, for as Hubert Jedin, the historian of Trent, has said, "Truth is reached in any community by means of an exchange of opinions, by arguments for and against, that is, by means of an intellectual struggle."[18] And the acute stage of the struggle in this instance opened on February 6, 1869, when the *Civiltà Cattolica* published under the heading of 'Correspondence from France,' a report alleged to represent French opinion on the forthcoming meeting. When the opponents of the new ultramontanism read that the majority of French Catholics felt that the Council would be as brief as Chalcedon in 451, which lasted less than a month, that it was their wish that the propositions of the *Syllabus of Errors* should be defined, and that they were likewise calling for a definition of our Lady's assumption, it was evident that there was going to be trouble. But what caused the greatest sensation was the statement that insofar as papal infallibility was concerned, it was hoped "that the unanimous manifestation of the Holy Spirit through the mouth of the Fathers

---

[17] AAB, 36A-E-11, Corcoran to Spalding, Rome, May 21, 1869. At the time Corcoran was reading with much admiration the recent work of the Bishop of Mainz, Wilhelm von Ketteler, *Deutschland nach dem Kriege von 1866* (Mainz, 1867), which had been written to give courage to the Austrian Catholics after their severe defeat by Prussia. "He treats fully and fearlessly of the present state of things," remarked Corcoran, "and gives indirectly some very good advice to the powers that be and to the future Council."
[18] *Ecumenical Councils of the Catholic Church. An Historical Outline* (New York, 1960), p. 234.

of the future ecumenical council will define it by acclamation."[19]
It is little wonder that one historian of the Council should have
characterized the *Civiltà's* article as "the sign of battle."[20]

Through the ensuing spring and summer and into the autumn
the party lines among the bishops were gradually taking shape.
By August an anonymous tract highly critical of the tactics of
the infallibilists was in wide circulation, and in the following
month the twenty bishops of Germany met at Fulda and revealed
their anxiety over developments such as that adumbrated by the
article in the *Civiltà Cattolica.* So worried were they, in fact, that
fourteen of them signed a letter to Pius IX expressing the conviction that a definition of infallibility would be inopportune.
Among these was Wilhelm von Ketteler of Mainz who in his
early years had been one of the strongest promoters of papal interests among the German Catholics. But von Ketteler's keen
sense of the role of the bishops in the direction of the Church had
taken a jolt in recent years. For example, Pius IX's definition of
the immaculate conception in 1854 had prompted him to tell
Dupanloup of Orléans:

> assemblies of bishops uniquely held for the purpose of providing a
> brilliant aspect to certain major festivities or to give formal approval
> of decisions already made in advance without having shared in their
> formulation—such assemblies displease me.[21]

As a result, in the Council von Ketteler was a stout inopportunist,
the name given to those opposed to the definition of papal infallibility, as he came to realize more fully how far off the mark
had been the words of the pastoral letter that he had published
on the eve of his departure for Rome. In that document he had
expressed his belief that all major definitions *de fide* must be made
by what he called "the unity of the whole episcopal magisterium,
not through an approximate majority," and that these decisions

---

[19] *Civiltà Cattolica,* V, 7th Series (February 6, 1869), 352.
[20] Butler, *op. cit.,* I, 108.
[21] Fritz Vigener, *Ketteler, Ein deutsches Bischofsleben des 19. Jahrhunderts*
(Munchen und Berlin, 1924), p. 569, n. 1. The writer is indebted for this and the
following reference to his friend and colleague, John K. Zeender, associate professor of modern history in The Catholic University of America.

should be made in council "either with the absolute unity of the assembled bishops or with a majority which is equivalent to unity. . . ."[22]

Meanwhile as the German hierarchy had shown a division of opinion at Fulda in September, 1869, between men like von Ketteler on the one side as against Ignaz Senestréy, Bishop of Regensburg, on the other, so the hierarchies of other countries, with the exception of Hungary, showed hardly any more real unity either before the Council's opening or thereafter. As von Ketteler had passed from the ultramontanist ranks to those of the inopportunists, so also did others change their ground, as, for example, Spalding, who left Baltimore an inopportunist, but who became so aroused after observing at Rome what he regarded as the unfair methods employed by the minority party that he ended an ardent infallibilist. Yet the switch of the titular leader of the American hierarchy in no way influenced the conduct of men like Augustin Verot, the Sulpician Bishop of Savannah (he was transferred to the new See of St. Augustine on March 11, 1870), whose candid criticisms on that and other matters earned him the name of *l'enfant terrible* of the Council, of Michael Domenec, C.M., Bishop of Pittsburgh, whose adhesion to the infallibility decree after all was over was so long delayed that there was considerable relief in orthodox quarters when it arrived a year and a half after the Council, and of Peter Richard Kenrick, Archbishop of St. Louis, described by one historian as, "perhaps the stiffest opponent of the definition."[23]

---

[22] Pastoral letter of November 12, 1869, John Michael Raich (Ed.) *Wilhelm Emmanuel Freiherr von Ketteler, Bischof von Mainz. Hirtenbriefe* (Mainz, 1904), pp. 600-601. For the inopportunist views of another German prelate cf. the letters of Gustav Adolf Cardinal von Hohenlohe, brother of the Bavarian foreign minister, who felt isolated in the ultramontanist atmosphere of the Roman Curia. He was anxious to have either Ignaz Döllinger or Johannes Friedrich, two priest-professors of the University of Munich with strongly anti-infallibilist views, sent to him as theologians for the Council. Cf. George W. Chrystal (Editor of English Edition), *Memoirs of Prince Chlodwig of Hohenlohe-Schillingsfuerst* edited by Friedrich Curtius (New York, 1906), I, 364-365; 369-374. Hereafter this work will be referred to as: Hohenlohe, *Memoirs*.

[23] Butler, *op. cit.*, II, 176. For the Americans cf. Raymond J. Clancy, C.S.C., "American Prelates in the Vatican Council," *Historical Records and Studies,* XXVIII (1937), 7-135. Ullathorne of Birmingham found the Americans in

An analysis of the positions taken by the bishops of other countries, both before and during the Council, would in general produce a similar picture to that of the Americans. For example, while the infallibilist views of Paul Cardinal Cullen, Archbishop of Dublin, were shared by a majority of the Irish bishops, that did not move men like John MacHale, Archbishop of Tuam, and David Moriarty, Bishop of Kerry, from the firmly inopportunist stand which they maintained to the end.[24] Nor did the sharp and forceful action of the titular leader of the English prelates, Henry Edward Manning, Archbishop of Westminster, in the least frighten William J. Clifford, Bishop of Clifton, who outdistanced all his countrymen in his opposition to papal infallibility. From the very first, of course, no one had been in any doubt about the man who did more than any other to shape the mind of France against the definition, and here Félix Dupanloup, Bishop of Orléans, had ranged on his side an impressive group of French prelates, including Georges Darboy, Archbishop of Paris, who, less than a year after the final vote, would lose his life at the hands of the Paris Commune (May 24, 1871). Moreover, in the case of the French there was likewise a fairly large middle group led by Henri-Marie Cardinal de Bonnechose, Archbishop of Rouen, who remained for some time uncommitted on the great question.

Meanwhile, what was the state of opinion in the world outside the Church? In certain foreign offices the prospect of a council had aroused alarm, and the first to give expression to this state of mind was the Foreign Minister of Bavaria, Prince Chlodwig

---

general "able and businesslike" and having "a great affection and respect" for Newman (Butler, *op. cit.*, I, 211). Ullathorne thought the Spanish-born Vincentian, Thaddeus Amat, Bishop of Monterey-Los Angeles "the shrewdest man in the Council . . . and he never speaks above a few minutes, but he hits the nail on the head invariably. He neither argues, nor talks, but simply proposes amendments on the text and comes down again." (*Ibid.*, II, 113).

[24] For a recent brief treatment cf. Peadar Mac Suibhne, "Ireland at the Vatican Council," *Irish Ecclesiastical Record*, 5th Series, XCIII (April, 1960), 209-222; (May, 1960), 295-307. In addition to the customary sources, this writer had access to the diary of James A. Goold, Bishop of Melbourne, and the papers of Nicholas Power, Coadjutor Bishop of Killaloe. It is amusing to find the bishop from Australia as late as 1870 referring to two American bishops as "from the colonies" (p. 303).

von Hohenlohe, whose brother was a cardinal in curia. On April 9, Hohenlohe sent a note to the powers, which had been prompted by the *Civiltà Cattolica's* article of the previous February, mention of which has already been made. Characterizing the Jesuit journal as "a semi-official organ" of the Holy See, he went on to say that it had recently declared it a duty for the Council to transform what he termed "the damnatory judgments" of the *Syllabus of Errors* into "positive decisions." Since some of these propositions were directed against what the prince called "important axioms of State organisation" that all civilized people had come to take for granted, he maintained that the governments were now confronted with a situation, which he described in these words:

> whether and in what form they would have to advise either the Bishops subject to their authority, or, at a later stage, the Council itself of the perilous consequences to which such a deliberate and fundamental disturbance of the relations of Church and State must inevitably lead.[25]

That Hohenlohe's concern was shared by others, there was no doubt. His note was the subject of a tense cabinet meeting at Downing Street where Prime Minister Gladstone, his mind colored by the biased reports reaching him from Sir John Acton at Rome, moved for a demonstration by the powers. Fortunately, the foreign secretary, the Earl of Clarendon, in closer touch with the true state of affairs through the despatches of Odo Russell, unofficial British agent at Rome, felt that English policy would be best served by the government's remaining aloof. In the end Clarendon won, and the threat to the Council's freedom that some had hoped might be initiated at London was removed. Gladstone's fears concerning the evil effect that the Council might have on the civil allegiance of British Catholics, nonetheless, grew stronger with the passing months, but in a somewhat resigned air he confessed to Archbishop Manning, "the prevailing opinion is that it is better to let those influences take their course, and work

---

[25] Hohenlohe, *Memoirs,* I, 327; the full text of the note is given here, pp. 326-328.

out the damage which will naturally and surely entail upon the see of Rome and upon what is bound to it."[26]

In Berlin, needless to say, no sympathy for the Council and its promoters was entertained by Bismarck and his colleagues. Yet, as he told Hohenlohe when the latter visited him in early June, while in general he agreed with his views, he would propose that the German states take joint and secret action to deprecate at Rome what he called "too sweeping measures," rather than to make any official protest.[27] As for Austria-Hungary, the Protestant chancellor, Count Friedrich Ferdinand von Beust, had replied to Hohenlohe's original note, that since the Vienna government espoused the principle of religious freedom, it could hardly be said to have accepted its consequences were it to attempt any "preventive and restrictive measures," as he termed them, concerning so fundamental a part of the constitution of the Catholic

---

[26] Gladstone to Manning, April 16, 1870, John Morley, *The Life of William Ewart Gladstone* (New York, 1903), II, 511. Gladstone felt that the American bishops were in the best position to prevent the worst from happening in the Council. He told Lord Acton: "Of all the prelates at Rome, none have a finer opportunity, to none is a more crucial test now applied, than to those of the United States. For if there, where there is nothing of covenant, of restraint or of equivalent between the church and the state, the propositions of the Syllabus are still to have the countenance of the episcopate, it becomes really a little difficult to maintain in argument the civil rights of such persons to toleration, however conclusive be the argument of policy in favour of granting it." (*Ibid.*, II, 511, n.d., n.p.). For further details and correspondence touching the crucial London cabinet meeting of April, 1869, cf. Edmund Sheridan Purcell, *Life of Cardinal Manning, Archbishop of Westminster* (New York, 1896), II, 433 ff.

[27] Hohenlohe's diary, June 12, 1869, Hohenlohe, *Memoirs*, I, 346-347. In the following spring when, according to Bismarck, the press asked the government to support those German bishops who were in opposition to the Roman Curia's conciliar policies, he asked how this was to be done, discounted any such attempt, and then stated: "We cannot take preventive measures as they would be of no value, but it is open to us to adopt a repressive policy in case a decision is come to in opposition to our wishes." This statement is given under date of March 21, 1870, in Moritz Busch, *Bismarck, Some Secret Pages of His History* (London, 1898), I, 20. A few days later chagrin at the progress of the infallibilists prompted Bismarck to suggest a conference of the powers as being, perhaps, useful; even if it could no longer hope to influence the Council, something might be gained by considering "how far the injurious effects of its decisions on the peace of Church and State could be minimised." (*Ibid.*, I, 22). Daru, however, turned down the idea and Beust would not act; with the Catholic powers thus declining to move, Bismarck fell back on the policy of supporting the efforts made by the German bishops to prevent what were styled "illegal changes" in the Church's constitution and "to preserve both Church and State from a disturbance of the peace." (*Ibid.*, I, 24).

Church as an ecumenical council. As for the fears for the State which Hohenlohe foresaw from the Council, Beust remarked, "We can neither affirm nor deny the imminence of such a danger."[28] Nor did a visit from Hohenlohe to Vienna in late August bring Beust around. He shared entirely the Bavarian foreign minister's views about the evil being done by the ultramontanist churchmen; but he was resting his hope that something might be gained by a split in the Austrian hierarchy which, he said, "would not come to pass unless the Government maintained a completely passive attitude."[29]

Thus the first major attempt of outside intervention in the Council came to nothing. Six months later the threat was revived by the liberal Catholic, Comte Napoleon Daru, Foreign Minister of France, whose independent action in sending a somewhat menacing note to Rome on February 20, 1870, not only startled the cabinet of Emile Ollivier, but touched off a chain of events that so frightened Giacomo Cardinal Antonelli, Secretary of State, that he called together his principal supporters among the cardinals, and on March 25 they went in a body to Pius IX to beg him to withdraw the infallibility question from the Council. But the Pope would not yield, and in the end the second and final threat passed when its chief instigator, Daru, resigned from the cabinet on April 22 over a difference on domestic issues with the Emperor Napoleon III. At this juncture Ollivier, well disposed toward the Church and friendly toward Pio Nono, took over the foreign ministry, immediately reversed Daru's policy, and the episode was closed with the despatch of a telegram from Paris to Rome that read, "*Daru se retire, Ollivier remplace, Concile*

---

[28] Beust to Count Friedrich von Ingelheim, Austrian Minister to Bavaria, Vienna, May 15, 1869, Hohenlohe, *Memoirs,* I, 335. Actually, Hohenlohe had not proposed any 'preventive and restrictive measures,' but had only asked for Beust's views.

[29] Hohenlohe's diary, August 25, 1869, *ibid.,* I, 363. Beust was quoted as placing hope in Maximilian von Tarnoczy, Archbishop of Salzburg, "as a Liberal." In the end the Austrian bishops split over infallibility, even though it was not in a way to fulfill Beust's expectations, with Josef Rauscher and Friedrich Schwarzenberg, the Cardinal Archbishops of Vienna and Prague, respectively, among the strongest inopportunists; while Vincenz Gasser, Prince Bishop of Brixen, was an ultramontanist and Josef Fessler, Bishop of St. Polten, secretary of the Council, a moderate infallibilist.

libre."[30] Free, indeed, it was, and that curiously enough by the grace of a Protestant premier of France who seven years later would publish a history of the Vatican Council about which the leading English historian of that gathering would remark that, of all the books he had read, "this one comes perhaps the nearest to the ideal of historical objectivity and impartiality."[31]

That brings us to the great debate itself where in an abbreviated form we shall hope to see what the Council had in the meantime done with its freedom. It is doubtful that any event in the history of the modern Church ever gave rise to a greater flow of misinformation than the Vatican Council. This misinformation, both accidental and deliberate, not only rendered accurate knowledge of what was transpiring almost impossible for those outside, but at times it seriously darkened the minds of those within the council chamber. This circumstance not only later made the historian's task of disentangling the web of error, misunderstanding and misinterpretation an exceedingly difficult one, but at the time it contributed mightily to the bitter spirit in which prelates of opposing opinions at times fought their battles. As usually happens when feeling runs high, on both sides men gave voice to absurdities, and that both in public and in private. In the earlier stages of the neo-ultramontanist enthusiasm, for example, Gaspard Mermillod, later to be Bishop of Lausanne and Geneva and a cardinal, preached a sermon which he entitled, "The Three Incarnations of the Son of God," wherein he described the divine action as having taken place "in the womb of a virgin, in the eucharist, and in the old man of the Vatican."[32] But this piece of theological nonsense was more than matched by the malice and virulence against the pontiff's person and official prerogatives that began to appear in the *Allgemeine Zeitung* of Augsburg in March, 1869, chiefly from the pen of the learned priest-scholar, Ignaz Döllinger, professor of church history in the University of Munich, writing under the name of 'Janus.' Bishop

---

[30] Butler, *op. cit.*, II, 25.

[31] *Ibid.*, I, 100. Butler called Ollivier's explanation and defense of the *Syllabus of Errors*, "the best—better than Dunpanloup's, better than Newman's." (*Ibid.*, I, 101).

[32] Aubert, *op. cit.*, p. 303.

Ullathorne was amply justified, therefore, in warning his priests and people in a lenten pastoral letter against these falsehoods where, as he said:

> designs are attributed to the Council of which the Council knows nothing; and bishops are invested with views and notions, and are described as taking this or that course of action, which are utterly unbefitting their characters, and are often in direct opposition to their real sentiments.[33]

Yet the situation continued unrelieved to the end, and years afterward fantastic stories about certain churchmen were still in circulation and being believed.[34]

Although the formal opening of the Vatican Council had taken place on December 8, 1869, for many weeks little or no real progress was made. In fact, up to the following March 18 not a single decree had yet been enacted. Prolonged discussions continued week by week on a universal catechism, on reform of the breviary, on priests' retreats and other aspects of clerical life and discipline, while simultaneously extensive debates were conducted on the elements entering into the definition of Catholic faith. But the bishops were not to be hurried, nor were some of them easily to be pleased. Nearly two months after the sessions had begun Ullathorne gave Newman a vivid description of the pace of business when he stated that if the Oratorian could see, as he expressed it, "schemata brought in, only to be pulled to pieces and sent out again, bleeding in every limb," he would realize that

[33] Pastoral letter of Ullathorne from Rome, February 10, 1870, Butler, *op. cit.,* I, 255. After the 'Janus' letters came out in book form as *The Pope and the Council* in July, 1869, Ullathorne stated on October 22, "It is the gravest and severest attack on the Holy See and the Jesuits, and especially on the policy of Rome for a thousand years, and will be a great storehouse for the adversaries of the Church." (*Ibid.,* I, 111).

[34] One of the most egregious examples of this bias was the article of Lord Acton, "The Vatican Council," in the *North British Review,* LIII (October, 1870), 183-229. Acton's scholarly training might have been expected to preserve him from this sort of thing, but such was not the case. Moreover, it was Acton—and Döllinger—who were in no small measure responsible for agitating Gladstone against the Holy See and the Council. Cf. his pamphlet, *The Vatican Decrees in Their Bearing on Civil Allegiance: A Political Expostulation,* which was published in London in November, 1874, and by the end of the year had sold 145,000 copies.

in the end what he termed "party views and idiosyncracies" would be forced to yield before the consensus of the fathers.[35] Under these circumstances it was hardly to be wondered at that the *Dei Filius* on Catholic faith should not have been enacted until April 14; but when the final vote came that constitution's four chapters received the unanimous assent of the 667 bishops present. The catechism, the breviary, and like topics, however, were not so fortunate; and in the sequel they were lost to view.

All the while the shadow of the infallibility issue hung over the assembly. Through December those intent upon its definition worked steadily, and in secret, to rally support, and by the first days of the new year this majority party, as it was called, felt sufficiently strong to move into the open as the petitions circulating among the bishops for the question's introduction into the Council accumulated the necessary signatures. Through January and February frantic efforts to influence one way or another Pio Nono, the presiding cardinals, and the uncommitted bishops, filled the Roman air with the excitement of secret intrigues, tactical maneuvers, and sharp personal encounters. But the minority party was playing a losing game, for in opposition to the 380 names signed to the petition to bring on the question, they could muster only 140. It was not enough to block the majority party's plans, and on March 6, therefore, the public announcement was made that the infallibility question was coming before the Council.

There followed a period that gave evidence, on both sides, of deep searching of souls and at times of notable displays of courage in response to the voice of conscience, as well as an occasional revelation of actions unworthy of so high a cause. Among the minority's outside sympathizers was Newman, who from the outset had opposed the definition. He was kept in close touch with events by the lengthy accounts of the proceedings that reached him regularly from the Bishop of Birmingham. It was in reply, in late January, to such a letter that Newman, in the deepest confidence, laid bare for Ullathorne his inmost thoughts on the subject. Referring to the fears then current from the exaggerated news stories coming out of Rome, he said:

---

[35] Ullathorne to Newman, Rome, February 4, 1870, Butler, *op. cit.,* I, 217.

I look with anxiety at the prospect of having to defend decisions which may not be difficult to my private judgment, but may be most difficult to defend logically in the face of historical facts. What have we done to be treated as the Faithful never were treated before? When has definition of doctrine *de fide* been a luxury of devotion and not a stern painful necessity? Why should an aggressive and insolent faction be allowed to make the hearts of the just to mourn whom the Lord hath not made sorrowful? Why can't we be let alone when we have pursued peace and thought no evil?[36]

Incredible as it may seem, this letter got out of Ullathorne's possession and was published in the newspapers. Differences of this kind naturally engendered critical comment about those in the opposite camp as, for example, Bishop Moriarty of Kerry who as a member of the minority, which he styled the Church militant, remarked of the majority:

It is composed of men who have not come into conflict with the unbelieving mind, or into contact with the intellectual mind of the time. When I read the school of theology in which they were trained I am not surprised that they treat every doubter as a heretic.[37]

Yet in spite of the participants' conflicting views, and of the depth of feeling that at times motivated their expression, on the whole, the conciliar debates were conducted with dignity and moderation; and those governing the procedure acted with objectivity and fairness. Only once, on March 22, was there a scene when Joseph Strossmayer, Bishop of Diakovár, was the principal in a disorderly exchange with Anniballe Cardinal Capalti over the decree then under discussion attributing errors to Protestants of which the Bosnian bishop felt they were not guilty. There was likewise one serious breach of fairness when no provision was made for a representative of the minority on the commission *de fide;* and once Pio Nono, whose heart was clearly set on the definition, resorted to unfair tactics when he administered a severe rebuke to the distinguished Dominican theologian, Filippo Cardinal Guidi, Archbishop of Bologna, for his speech on June 18

---

[36] Newman to Ullathorne, Birmingham, January 28, 1870, Ward, *Newman*, II, 288.

[37] Moriarty to Newman, Rome, February 3, 1870, Butler, *op. cit.*, II, 29.

which sided with the minority party. In fact, there were even moments of high amusement, as on January 27 when Verot of Savannah, during a debate on the morals of the clergy, demanded that priests not only avoid theatres but also hunting with weapons, and with that in mind he asked to have a paragraph embodying his idea added to the proposed canon which would contain the following sentence: "The wretched spectacle of a man of God wandering through the fields and highways in search of birds and beasts should never be shown the faithful."[38] Some bishops spoke at very great length, a factor that caused acute distress to many of the more aged prelates, especially when the heat of the Roman summer began to set in. Even during the winter months a session could be trying, as that on January 4 when Johann B. Greith, Bishop of St. Gall, made a speech that prompted Ullathorne to comment:

> We have got home from a meeting of the Council where we were almost stunned by a Swiss bishop, who spoke for an hour, and roared as if he were talking from one mountain to another against wind and thunder.[39]

Yet the cardinal presidents rarely cut the speakers off. In that connection, years later, Cardinal Gibbons, who was at the time the youngest bishop in the Council, reminisced about the freedom of speech that prevailed, and he remarked:

> I can safely say that neither in the British House of Commons, nor in the French Chambers, nor in the German Reichstag, nor in our American Congress would a wider liberty of debate be tolerated than was granted in the Vatican Council.[40]

The point made by the Cardinal of Baltimore was clearly illustrated by the debates on papal infallibility. After the public announcement of March 6, two more months were given to drafting the decrees, to private discussions thereon, and then to re-

---

[38] Mansi, *op. cit.,* L, 539.
[39] Quoted in Butler, *op. cit.,* I, 194.
[40] James Cardinal Gibbons, "Personal Reminiscences of the Vatican Council," *North American Review,* CCCCXLIX (April, 1894), 393.

vision of the drafts. Finally, on May 9 the revised text was presented to the Council, and four days later the great debate began and ran until June 3. During those three weeks sixty-five bishops, thirty-nine in favor and twenty-six opposed to defining the Pope's infallibility, were heard from the ambo. But the heat was now becoming oppressive, and there were growing signs of fatigue. A motion was circulated among the bishops, therefore, to apply a cloture to the general debate; and when the presidents asked the pleasure of the fathers, a large majority were for cloture, although the following day a minority of eighty protested this action. The debate on the text of each of the four chapters of the proposed constitution was still to come, however; and during the course of it, every conceivable aspect of the question was aired, culminating on July 11 in the exhaustive exposition by Vincenz Gasser, Prince-Bishop of Brixen, whose speech lasted a little under four hours.[41] After due consideration as well of the 144 amendments proposed to the chapter on infallibility, one of the Council's high moments arrived, with the vote scheduled for July 13.

By this time a good number of prelates had ceased to play any active role in the Council as may be illustrated by reference to the bishops from the United States.. As far back as March 15 the strong inopportunist opinions of certain Americans showed up when Peter Richard Kenrick of St. Louis, John B. Purcell of Cincinnati, and Edward Fitzgerald of Little Rock, joined in a protest against a report that the infallibility issue would be advanced out of its regular order on the agenda, and that at the next general congregation it would be carried without discussion. They could not believe that anyone but a madman would tolerate or approve such an action. "But we give notice . . ." they warned, "that if the impossible should happen, we would immediately leave the council, and make public the reason for our departure."[42] Although the sequel proved that their fears had been exaggerated, four months later a number of these same churchmen were still firmly opposed to the definition. On Wednesday, July 13, which

---

[41] Butler devoted a separate chapter to the Gasser speech (II, 134-148).
[42] Mansi, *op. cit.*, LI, 714.

one of the Council's historians calls its "crucial day,"[43] there were 601 bishops present for the trial ballot on the *Pastor aeternus* constitution as a whole. Of these 451 voted *placet,* eighty-eight *non-placet,* and sixty-two *placet juxta modum,* or acceptance of papal infallibility with reservations. And it is significant to recall that there were then about seventy-six bishops still in Rome who absented themselves from this session. On July 13 only the Hungarian delegation of fifteen bishops maintained a solid bloc against the definition, while the other hierarchies divided more or less along the lines of the Americans where fifteen voted *placet,* four *non-placet,* and five *placet juxta modum,* with twenty-one absent. On July 17 the minority party made its final and vain effort to win a compromise solution from Pius IX; whereupon fifty-five bishops sent a formal protest to the Pope against holding the fourth public session scheduled for the following day. They would not be present in the council chamber since, as they said:

> filial piety and reverence, which not long ago drew our spokesmen to the feet of Your Holiness, will not suffer us, in a cause so closely touching the person of Your Holiness, publicly and before a Father to say: *non-placet.* . . . We will return, therefore, without delay to our flocks. . . .[44]

Again using the Americans as illustrative of the action of most of the national hierarchies, this document bore the signatures of the Archbishop of St. Louis and the Bishops of Pittsburgh and St. Augustine. Of the forty-five Americans who had come to Rome the previous autumn, therefore, twenty had by now either departed for home or had absented themselves from the session of July 18 when the final vote was taken. On this occasion 533 bishops pronounced their *placet* to the definition of papal infallibility of whom twenty-four were Americans, while the two *non-placets* were registered by Luigi Riccio, Bishop of Cajazzo in southern Italy, and Edward Fitzgerald, Bishop of Little Rock, Arkansas. Students of church history are familiar with the dramatic character of the closing scene when a furious electric storm

---

[43] Butler, *op. cit.,* II, 149.
[44] Mansi, *op. cit.,* LII, 1325.

broke over Rome and so darkened the skies that large candles
had to be held close to Pio Nono so that he might see to read the
text of the *Pastor aeternus.* Some of the minority interpreted the
storm as a sign of divine displeasure at the definition of the Pope's
infallibility; but Archbishop Manning, the majority voice, was in
no way disconcerted by talk of this kind. "They forgot," he said,
"Sinai and the Ten Commandments."[45]

In conclusion, what were the general results of the Church's
twentieth ecumenical Council? Perhaps, they can best be summarized from the three-fold viewpoint of the papacy, the bishops,
and the secular governments. First, insofar as the newly defined
doctrine on the primacy and infallibility of the sovereign pontiff
was concerned, there could be little doubt that, generally speaking, the position of the Pope had been enhanced in the eyes of
the Catholic world. In a sense it was a culminating point in the
centralizing tendencies that had been discernible within the
Church since the early years of the century. In fact, some men of
our own generation, whose fundamental loyalty to the Holy See
is beyond question, feel that this tendency is still a living force.
As for the vast majority of Catholics in 1870, they had never
seriously questioned the fact that the Pope was infallible in his
judgments on faith and morals, even if they did not have the
theological acumen to explain what that meant. With the exception, therefore, of the Old Catholic group who followed the teaching of Döllinger and Friedrich and lapsed into schism in Germany,
Switzerland, and the Netherlands—the estimates of whose numbers vary so greatly as almost to defy accurate calculation—once
the doctrine had been defined, neither priests nor laity felt much
change in their traditional religious commitment. For example,
Newman, who all along had believed the doctrine himself but
had opposed its definition, remarked to a friend after he had read
the text, "I saw the new definition yesterday and am pleased at its
moderation. . ."[46] What made matters easier, and at least to some
degree disarmed the critics, was the sparing use made of the

---

[45] Henry Edward Manning, *The True Story of the Vatican Council,* 2nd ed.
(London, 1877), p. 147.
[46] Ward, *Newman,* II, 307.

prerogative by Pius IX and his successors, it having been employed in solemn manner only once in the last ninety years when in 1950 Pope Pius XII defined the assumption of our Lady. Thus the wild prophecies and anticipation of frequent definitions of extreme neo-ultramontanists like Louis Veuillot and William George Ward, which had repelled so many both within and outside the Church, were proven entirely false.

As for the bishops, the struggle of conscience in the case of some was clearly a severe one. We have already mentioned the delay of a year and a half before Bishop Domenec of Pittsburgh sent in his adhesion to the constitution *Pastor aeternus,* and that of the fiery bishop from Bosnia, Joseph Strossmayer, did not come through until December, 1872. But unlike earlier councils, in 1870 there were no episcopal defections such, for example, as Nicea when in June, 325, two bishops refused to sign the Nicene Creed and about eighty ultimately passed over to the Arians, or at Ephesus in 431 where thirty or more bishops refused to accept the hypostatic union of the two natures of Christ in the single person of the Word and to accord to our Lady the title of Mother of God. Obviously, the minority would have preferred that papal infallibility had not been defined at all, but with it a *fait accompli* even the bitterest foes ultimately gave way. Part of their chagrin and disappointment stemmed, incidentally, from the Council's failure to explore, let alone to reach any conclusion, about the bishops' place in the magisterium of the Church, a subject which some of their successors still feel should be clarified.

Finally, in regard to the secular governments, the immediate effects of the definition of papal infallibility were almost uniformly unhappy. As an indication of Austria's profound displeasure, Vienna repudiated its concordat of 1855 with the Holy See. In Germany the making of a quarrel between Church and State was already at hand and the definition heaped fuel upon the fire. The more that Bismarck, the iron chancellor of the new German Empire, thought about what had happened, the more alarmed and indignant he became, fancying, as he did, that the Pope's infallibility would lessen the State's assurance of allegiance of the German Catholics. That was the spirit in which he supported the *Kulturkampf* that broke over the German Church early in 1872, as it was the intent which in the course of the Reichstag debates on the religious question informed his famous boast of May 14 of that year, "Do not fear, we will not go to Canossa either in body or in spirit."[47]   As a consequence the German Catholics were to experience a decade of acute suffering before the State's persecution of the Church would finally be abandoned in the face of the dangerous peril of Socialism.

As for France, once the restraining hand of Marshall Marie Edmé de McMahon was removed in January, 1879, and the Third Republic was firmly launched under Jules Grévy, the French Church was to feel the full force of the most virulent anticlericalism, although it would be a mistake to attribute the ordeal of the French Catholics primarily to the definition of papal infallibility, for in all likelihood it would have befallen them in any case. Finally, the defeat of Gladstone and the Liberal Party in the elections of February, 1874, left him time to ruminate about the evils of the Vatican Council, to visit Döllinger in Munich in September of that year, and to come home to publish, two months later, the pamphlet that revived all the old English fears of papal aggression, even though it did call forth the notable replies concerning the *Syllabus of Errors* and papal infallibility of Archbishop Manning to the London *Times* and of John Henry Newman in the well-known *Letter Addressed to His Grace the Duke of Norfolk*. Although the controversy had, indeed, stirred up anew bitter debate, it had not provoked any crippling legislation such as occurred in Germany and France, and by the end of the decade, at least a surface tranquility had returned to English public life.

Let the last word here be said by the Archbishop of Westminster whose conduct during the assembly at Rome had been consistently vigilant, vigorous, and sharp, and not always answering to the rules of fairness to one's opponents. But even his most unrelenting enemies could not challenge Manning's sincerity in so forcefully urging the definition, and with the hindsight afforded by

---

[47] C. Grant Robertson, *Bismarck* (London, 1918), p. 316.

the long interval that separates us from those exciting days of 1870, it is apparent that the words which he used in retrospect to describe the Council could hardly be gainsaid. He stated:

> . . . in due time it will be perceived that never was any council so numerous, nor were ever the dissentient voices relatively so few; that never was any council so truly ecumenical both in its representation and in its acceptance; that never were the separations after it fewer, feebler, or more transient; and that never did the Church come out from a great conflict more confirmed in its solidity, or more tranquil in its internal peace.[48]

Right Reverend John Tracy Ellis

---

[48] Manning, *op. cit.*, pp. 207-208.

The Theology of the General Council

The Theology of the General Council

In the present organization of scholastic theology, the treatise on the nature and the authority of the ecumenical council belongs within the field of fundamental dogma. Basically, fundamental dogma constitutes, as it were, the introduction to sacred theology. It is the section dealing with the nature and the competence of this science, its various sources and the basic body of truth with which it is concerned. Thus, within the area of fundamental dogmatic theology, we find the introduction to theology most properly so-called, the treatise on revelation, which is better known as the science (as distinct from the art) of apologetics, and the treatise *de locis theologicis,* the part concerned with the sources employed in sacred theology.

The classical listing of these sources is that contained in the work *De locis theologicis,* written by the Dominican Melchior Cano, who died in 1560. The book enumerates and describes ten of these *loci.* They are:

1) the authority of Sacred Scripture; 2) the authority of the traditions of Christ and of the apostles; 3) the authority of the Catholic Church; 4) the authority of the councils, especially of the general (or ecumenical) councils, in which the authority of the Catholic Church is found; 5) the authority of the Roman Church, which, by divine privilege, is and is called Apostolic; 6) the authority of the ancient Saints (or the Fathers) of the Church; 7) the authority of the scholastic theologians, to whom Cano joins the experts in canon law; 8) natural reason, which is most widely manifest throughout all the sciences; 9) the authority of the philosophers, among whom Cano reckons the experts in the field of civil law; 10) the authority of human history.[1]

---

[1] Cano, *De locis theologicis,* lib. I, c. 3, in Migne's *Theologiae Cursus Completus,* I, col. 62.

Historically, three of these sources have always been considered together since the middle of the fifteenth century, when Cardinal John de Turrecremata wrote his famous *Summa de ecclesia.*[2] This work is divided into four books. The first deals with the universal Church. The second is concerned with the Roman Church, or with the primacy of its pontiff. The third treats of universal councils and their authority. The fourth and final book of this *Summa de ecclesia* is divided into two parts. The first of these deals with schism and schismatics, while the other is a treatise on heresy and heretics. It is the most important source book for the theology of the ecumenical council.

The *Summa de ecclesia* was finished in October, 1453. It was destined to be the work in which the actual theological treatise on the Catholic Church would realize its most perfect form.

It must be definitely understood that the *Summa de ecclesia* was not, strictly speaking, a work in the field of *scholastic* theology. Scholastic theology as such had been in existence since the twelfth century, when the *Four Books of Sentences* of Peter the Lombard had expressed the teaching that was destined to comprise the content of what was taught as theology in the universities and the schools. There is no treatise on the Church, no treatise on the Roman pontiff, and no treatise on the ecumenical councils in the master work of Peter the Lombard. Furthermore, such treatises are not contained in the *Summa theologica* of St. Thomas Aquinas, the text that would come to supplant the *Four Books of Sentences* as the basic manual of the theological schools.

During the early period of scholasticism, however, there had been a great deal of writing on the Church, on the sovereign pontiff, and on the ecumenical council, by trained scholastic teachers. Simply to list a few examples, there was the work of Moneta of Cremona, the *Five Books against the Cathari and the Waldensians.*[3] Moneta was a thirteenth-century Dominican

---

[2] The book was written 1448-1449, and was first printed in 1480.

[3] The *Adversus Catharos et Valdenses Libri Quinque* was written about 1244, and was printed at Rome in 1743.

theologian. Another thirteenth-century Dominican theologian, St. Thomas Aquinas, set down what was going to become the foundation for the treatise on the notes of the Church in his short *Commentary on the Creed*.[4] Similarly the basic statement of the truth about the position of the Roman pontiff in the Church militant of the New Testament is presented in St. Thomas's book *Contra errores Graecorum*.[5]

In the early years of the fourteenth century there had been some highly important writings in this field. Very prominent among them were the *De regimine chrisiano*[6] of the Augustinian, James of Viterbo, and the *De planctu eccelsiae*[7] of the Franciscan, Alvaro Pelayo. And, in the early part of the fifteenth century, there was important teaching on the Church and on the Roman pontiff in the *Antiquitatum fidei catholicae ecclesiae doctrinale* of the great English Carmelite, Thomas Netter of Walden.[8]

None of these writings belongs to the field of scholastic theology, strictly so-called. All of them, with the exception of St. Thomas's *Commentary on the Creed,* are primarily controversial in tone. Moneta wrote against the Albigensians and the Waldensians. St. Thomas was concerned with the errors of the dissident oriental Christians. James of Viterbo set out to defend the papacy against the attacks of Philip the Fair of France. Alvaro

---

[4] St. Thomas wrote: *"Haec autem Ecclesia sancta habet quatuor conditiones, quia est una, quia est sancta, quia est catholica, id est, universalis, et quia est fortis et firma."* He likewise teaches that the firmness and strength of the Church come from the fact that it is founded on Our Lord and on the Apostles, and that *"inde est quod dicitur Ecclesia apostolica"* (*ad verba "Sanctam Ecclesiam catholicam"* in the *Expositio super Symbolo Apostolorum scilicet Credo in Deum*). St. Thomas also defines the Church as the *"congregatio fidelium,"* and says *"quilibet Christianus est membrum ipsius Ecclesiae"* (*ibid.*).

[5] The last portion of the *Contra Errores Graecorum ad Urbanum IV Papam Maximum* contains a teaching about the primacy of the Roman pontiff which is the same as that defined in the First Vatican Council's constitution *Pastor Aeternus.*

[6] The treatise *De regimine christiano* was written in 1301-1302 and was dedicated to Pope Boniface VIII. A critical edition of the text is to be found in Arquillière's *Le plus ancien traité de l'Église: Jacques de Viterbe, De regimine christiano (1301-1302).* The work was published in Paris by Beauchesne in 1926.

[7] The *De planctu Ecclesiae* was composed at the court of Avignon between 1320 and 1330. Alvaro Pelayo was a student of Duns Scotus.

[8] The first two parts of this eminently useful work were praised by Pope Martin V during the summer of 1427.

Pelayo directed his attack against the erroneous teachings of Marsilius of Padua and John of Jandun. And, of course, Netter defended Catholic teaching against the misrepresentations of the followers of Wyclif.

It was the glory of Cardinal John de Turrecremata, in his *Summa de ecclesia,* once and for all to gather together, from the field of polemical theology, and particularly from the field of canon law, the elements which were to form the scholastic treatise on the Church, on the sovereign pontiff, and on the ecumenical councils.

Interestingly enough, what the *Summa de ecclesia* has to say with reference to the Roman pontiff and the ecumenical council is just about what is to be found in the best contemporary theological writings on these subjects. And what this same work has to say about the nature of the Church itself is what the best efforts in scholastic eccelesiology today are trying to reproduce in the teaching of this science.

Over the course of the centuries there has been a great deal of change in the content and in the arrangement of the theological treatise on the Church. Indeed, it is safe to say that there is not another section in all the field of scholastic theology in which there has been as much rearrangement and reordering as there has been in the field of ecclesiology. Of course there is not and there has not been any thesis which was once rejected as false which is now accepted as certain or even as probable. And, by the same token, there is no thesis which was once accepted as certain which is now rejected. But by reason of the various ways in which the *tractatus de ecclesia* has been handled during the course of the centuries, problems have arisen about just what truths should be included in this portion of sacred theology. And it seems quite obvious that today the trend is to reorganize this section quite in line with the procedure adopted by Cardinal John de Turrecremata in his *Summa de ecclesia.*

The study of the vicissitudes of the theological treatise on the Catholic Church, from the time it came to maturity outside of the fabric of scholastic theology in Turrecremata's *Summa de ecclesia,* down through the years of the counter-Reformation literature, at the hands of masters like Latomus,[9] Driedo,[10] St. Robert Bellarmine,[11] and Francis Sylvius,[12] who treated it pre-eminently as a part of controversial, as distinct from scholastic, theology, down through the first efforts made by men like Bannez,[13] Suarez,[14] and Gregory of Valentia,[15] and Tanner,[16] and Wiggers,[17] to incorporate this treatise into the framework of scholastic theology, is one of the most interesting and important tasks facing the historian of sacred theology in our times.

---

[9] Latomus (+ 1544) wrote on this subject in his *De primatu Romani Pontificis adversus Lutherum; Ejusdem responsio ad Elleboron Joannis Oecolampadii; Ejusdem responsio ad Lutherum qua se defendit, quia ex Summi Pontificis et Caesaris mandatis passi sunt libros Lutheri cremari Lovanii et ideo illos incendiarios vocat,* and in his *De confessione secreta; de quaestionum generibus quibus Ecclesia certat intus et foris; de Ecclesia et humanae legis obligatione.*

[10] Driedo (+ 1535) made an extraordinary contribution to the development of ecclesiology in his *De ecclesiasticis scripturis et dogmatibus libri IV.*

[11] It is important to see how St. Robert Bellarmine arranged his teaching on the Church and on its councils in the masterpiece *De controversiis christianae fidei adversus huius temporis haereticos,* which was first published in 1584. The matter with which we are concerned is to be found in the first two volumes of this work. The first volume contains three *Controversiae generales,* the first entitled *De Verbo Dei,* the second, *De Christo Capite totius Ecclesiae,* and the third, *De Summo Pontifice.* The second volume contains four *Controversiae generales.* The first is *De Conciliis et Ecclesia.* The second is *De membris Ecclesiae,* the third *De Ecclesia quae purgatur in locis subterraneis,* and the fourth, *De Ecclesia quae triumphat in coelis.*

[12] Sylvius' *Libri sex de praecipuis fidei nostrae orthodoxae controversiis cum nostris haereticis* was published in 1638 and was a magnificent contribution to the literature of sacred theology. The great Douai theologian divided his work into six books. The first five of these deal with the first five of the *loci theologici* of Melchior Cano, but Sylvius treats his material in great detail and much more effectively than Cano. The sixth book deals with sixth and the seventh of Cano's *loci theologici.*

[13] Bannez (+ 1604) placed his treatises on the Church, the Roman pontiff, and the councils as an appendix to his commentary on St. Thomas's *Summa theologica,* IIa-IIae, q. 1, art. 10. As a matter of fact there are two such treatises on the Church in his *Scholastica commentaria in secundam secundae Angelici Doctoris D. Thomae.* The first is meant for beginners, and the other for more advanced students.

[14] Suarez placed his treatises on the Church, the Pope, and the councils in his *Opus de triplici virtute theologica,* in the section *De fide.*

[15] Gregory of Valentia allocated these treatises in his *Commentaria theologica* also in the section *De fide.*

[16] Adam Tanner likewise carried this group of treatises as an appendix to the section *De fide* in his *Theologica scholastica.*

[17] John Wiggers carries this teaching under the general heading *De fide* in his *Commentaria de virtutibus theologicis.*

It so happens that the treatise on the Church which was incorporated into the framework of scholastic theology was not the work as it had been formulated by Turrecremata, but as it had been elaborated by counter-Reformation controversialists like Peter Soto, Stapleton, St. Robert, and Sylvius. And it is essential to realize that these men were interested in bringing out, not the relatively complete documentation on the nature of the Church that was set forth in the *Summa de ecclesia,* but only those sections of the true doctrine which had been denied or questioned by the reformers.

In our own library here at the University we have an example of this procedure in our copy of Soto's *Assertio Catholicae Fidei circa Articulos Confessionis Nomine Illustrissimi Ducis Wirtenbergensis Oblatae per Legatos eius Concilio Tridentino,* which, from a theological point of view, is perhaps the most interesting volume in the University's collection. In this volume (printed in Cologne, in 1555), the verso pages are divided into two columns. The first column is given over to the Protestant profession of belief, which Soto has set out to criticize. The other contains the Catholic contradictions to the statement appearing in this Protestant profession of belief. Thus, where there is, in the original Profession of the Duke of Würtemberg, some statement opposed to Catholic doctrine, the space in the column opposite this statement is devoted to the Catholic contradiction of the error. And, on the other hand, where the Protestant profession contains some statement which was in no way opposed to Catholic teaching, the space in the column opposite this statement is left blank.

The actual text of Soto's *Assertio Catholicae Fidei* is contained on the recto pages of this book. And in each case it is the development of the objections to the Protestant teaching set forth in the right-hand column of the verso page. And quite obviously, according to such an arrangement, there could not be, and as a matter of fact there was not, any detailed discussion in the text of the *Assertio Catholicae Fidei* of truths which were held by the Catholic Church and which were not denied by the Protestant professions of belief.

Thus it happened, to take simply the outstanding examples, that the theological doctrine on the Church set forth in the *Summa de ecclesia* of Turrecremata was not fully covered in the teaching on the Church presented in the *Controversies* of St. Robert Bellarmine and Francis Sylvius. But, what is most interesting from the point of view of the history of sacred theology, it was precisely the theological teaching on the Church as it was contained in the *Controversies* of St. Robert and of Sylvius, and not the more complete teaching on the Church as it was written up by Turrecremata, that first entered into the fabric of scholastic theology properly so-called.

The first men who attempted to insert the *tractatus de ecclesia* into the framework of scholastic theology tended to allocate this treatise, together with the treatises on the Roman pontiff and on the ecumenical councils, within an appendix, either to the treatise on faith as a whole, or to the commentary on St. Thomas's tenth article to his first question in the secunda-secundae of the *Summa theologica*. What they took over was the treatise on the Church much as it existed in the *Controversies* of St. Robert and of Sylvius. But the treatises on the Roman pontiff and on the councils, taken likewise from the stream of theological tradition most perfectly exemplified in the writings of Bellarmine and of Sylvius, had not been modified so drastically as had the treatise on the Church.

Definitely there are advances to be found, when we compare the teaching *de conciliis* in the *Summa de ecclesia* of Turrecremata with the same treatise found in the works of Bellarmine and Sylvius. But the fact of the matter is that the changes here are definitely advances. The teaching set forth in the sixteenth and seventeenth century manuals is manifestly clearer and more definite than what is expounded on the same subject in the *Summa de ecclesia*. Still there has not been anything like the advance or progress in the theology of the councils (or for that matter in the theology *de Romano Pontifice*) that there has been within the field of what was originally contained in the *tractatus de ecclesia Christi*.

This is true despite the fact that, during the course of the years, the *tractatus de ecclesia* has tended, in the literature of the theological manuals, to absorb the content of the other two treatises. Today if we examine the widely used manuals in fundamental dogmatic theology, we shall find that the material on the Roman pontiff (which is generally quite ample, but not always very adequate,) and the teaching on the ecumenical councils (which is all too frequently neither ample nor adequate) contained within the ambit of the *Tractatus de ecclesia Christi*. And this has come about, in great measure, because, particularly during the past two centuries, there was a tendency to fashion the treatise on the Church to fit the Procrustean bed of apologetics. What had already been abbreviated by the post-Reformation theologians who made it a controversial treatise directed against the Protestant reformers now became even more badly mishandled by men who tried to make this *tractaus de ecclesia Christi* into a portion of apologetics called the *demonstratio catholica*.

The net result of this tendency has been the comparative neglect of the *theological* treatise on the ecumenical councils. Over the course of the years there has been continued study of the *history* of these councils. And such study has been most providential for the Church. But, on the other hand, there has been comparatively little on the genuine *theology* of these councils. And very definitely there is a theology of the ecumenical councils which is not at all to be confused with the history of these gatherings, even though, as in all other portions of scholastic theology, history (and in this instance especially the history of the ecumenical councils) is one of the *loci theologici* which must be taken into consideration and which must be used as source material in any valid theological interpretation.

For this reason it is quite interesting to examine what the *Summa de ecclesia* has to say about the theology of the ecumenical council as such. It will be found that there is far more on this subject in this classical fifteenth-century manual than there is in most of the contemporary literature on this same subject. Yet, astonishingly enough, the very theses which are most characteristic of the contemporary writings on the theology of the ecumenical councils are to be found in Turrecremata's masterpiece.

In the very first chapter of his book, "On the Universal Councils and their Authority," Turrecremata defines the term "council," prescinding from the civic or the ecclesiastical character of such gatherings. For Turrecremata, a council is "the congregation or gathering of prudent men, called together by the public authority, to deal with common purpose with the things necessary for or helpful to the commonwealth or the group as a whole."[18] Such a definition, the author argues, takes cognizance of all four causes of such gatherings.

Quite in keeping with the ecclesiological spirit of his time, Turrecremata speaks of ecclesiastical councils as being held, according to the Scriptures, in the Church militant of the Old Testament as well as in that of the New. It is characteristic of the theological mentality of the time that the author of the *Summa de ecclesia* should take these words from the Vulgate Old Testament as indicating that the council was also an Old Testament ecclesiastical institution.[19] The second verse of the sixteenth chapter of the Book of Numbers speaks, after enumerating the leading figures in the rebellion of Core, of "*aliique filiorum Israel ducenti quinquaginta viri proceres synagogae et qui tempore concilii per nomina vocabantur.*" This was taken as an indication of the fact that, in the days of Moses, there were councils held in that company which, according to the dispensation of the Old Testament, constituted the chosen people or the *ecclesia* of God on earth.

Much more enlightening is the section of the *Summa de ecclesia* in which Turrecremata speaks of the origin of the councils in the Church militant of the New Testament. The author himself enumerates eight such councils or synods held during the time of the Apostles,[20] although he admits that the *Glossa ordinaria,* which together with the *Corpus iuris canonici* is the most important source for the *Summa de Ecclesia* after the Scripture it-

---

[18] Turrecremata, *Summa de ecclesia,* Lib. III, c. 1.
[19] Cf. *ibid.,* c. 2.
[20] Cf. *ibid.*

self, speaks of only four councils as having been held by the Apostles.

Turrecremata distinguishes between universal councils, provincial councils, and the diocesan synod.[21] Very interesting is his division of universal councils. He speaks of two kinds of such gatherings, those which are universal (he does not rely on the word "ecumenical") by reason of the universality of the men who are invited to the gathering or who actually take part in it, and those which are universal by reason of the universality of the authority it has to issue decrees binding on the entire Catholic Church.[22]

The first class of such universal councils is the group which theology and history today speak of as ecumenical councils. The second includes synods over which the sovereign pontiff himself presides, and which can speak with authority to the universal Church precisely by reason of the power and the responsibility over the universal Church which God has given to the successor of St. Peter.[23] And, while Turrecremata generally speaks of the first class of gatherings, the ones which are ecumenical councils in the strict sense of the term, he occasionally speaks of the other class of councils in the course of his exposition on the universal councils and their authority. He makes it clear that the first of the real ecumenical councils was that of Nicea, and then he goes on to speak of the Roman synods which were headed by the sovereign pontiff.

In dealing with the first class of universal councils, the ones which are properly designated as ecumenical councils, Turrecremata offers this definition: "The universal council of the Catholic Church is the congregation of the major prelates convoked by the special authority of the Roman Pontiff to deal solemnly and with common purpose with the Christian religion under the presidency of the Pope or of his delegate."[24] It is his

---

[21] Cf. *ibid.*, c. 3.

[22] Cf. *ibid.*, c. 4.

[23] Turrecremata thus envisioned an authority over the universal Church for a Roman synod or for a provincial council over which the sovereign pontiff presided, and at least the doctrinal decrees of which he had confirmed and promulgated.

[24] *Summa de ecclesia*, Lib. III, c. 5.

thesis that, "If anyone attentively reads the divine Scripture and the canons and the institutes of the sacred Fathers, he will clearly see that to call together a universal synod lies regularly within the competence of the authority of the Roman Pontiff alone."[25]

Turrecremata lists no less than twelve reasons which, in his view, have motivated the calling of universal councils of the Catholic Church. These are:

(1) In order that there may be more mature and effective deliberation about matters affecting the universal Church;

(2) So that there may be more solemn and more extensive authority for the repudiation of heresy and for the condemnation of heretics;

(3) To put an end to a schism;

(4) For the bringing back, or for the confutation, of heretics through the way of disputation;

(5) When great and powerful enemies face the Church;

(6) For the sake of asking from God guidance required for the proper direction of the Church;

(7) When grave danger or the threat of a great persecution faces the Church, and when the aid of the entire Church is considered requisite to deal with this problem;

(8) In order that the integrity or the solidity of the faith may be assured through a complete acceptance of the constitutions and the definitions issued by some preceding council (Logically, in the *Summa de ecclesia,* this reason would also take account of failure on the part of considerable numbers of the members of the Church to follow the doctrinal or the disciplinary decrees issued previously by one of the sovereign pontiffs.) ;

(9) In order to inquire into a suspicion of heresy directed against the Roman pontiff (Certainly neither Turrecremata nor any other reputable theologian who taught this same doctrine was thinking of any suspicion that a doctrine issued *ex cathedra* by the Roman pontiff could ever be heretical. But Turrecremata and the other ecclesiologists of the golden age were convinced that it was quite possible for a Pope to lapse into heresy as an individual, and thus to forfeit his position as a member of the Church,

[25] *Ibid.,* c. 6.

and obviously as the visible head of the Church militant. And, during the lifetime of Turrecremata, the councils of Pisa (1409), Constance (1414-1418), and Basle (1431-1443), had all issued declarations accusing of heresy men who were regarded as popes by great masses of the Catholic population. Pisa and Basle had actually made such accusations against men who are today regarded, and rightly regarded, as the rightful Bishops of Rome.) ;

(Thus this ninth reason for a universal council alleged here by the Cardinal John de Turrecremata does not in any way constitute a denial of papal infallibility [a doctrine which Turrecremata held as a dogma of divine faith].)

(10) In order to defend the Roman pontiff against attacks made against him;

(11) When there is grave doubt about the validity of a papal election;

(12) For a more efficacious, a more solemn, and a more universal reformation of the Church.[26]

Interestingly enough, Turrecremata offers examples of councils which have been called for each of these twelve different reasons. Speaking of the councils called for the second reason, the repudiation of heresy and the condemnation of heretics, he says that many councils have been called for that purpose "and especially the seven famous and principal ones." And he lists the eighth universal council, the famed anti-Photian gathering of 869-70, as one of the universal councils called for the extirpation of schism.[27]

The *Summa de ecclesia* was written after the close of the Council of Florence, the seventeenth ecumenical council according to the listing most in use in our own day. Yet, in the ninth chapter of the third book, the one he devotes to the nature and the authority of the universal councils, Turrecremata does not make any attempt to assign numbers to the ecumenical councils of the West. These are mentioned, of course, along with several councils over which the sovereign pontiff presided and which were, according to Turrecremata's reckoning, "universal" councils of the second class, universal, not in their membership, but only by

---

[26] Cf. *ibid.,* c. 9.
[27] Cf. *ibid.*

reason of the universal responsibility and authority of the Roman pontiff who was the supreme legislator within these gatherings.

When the *Summa de ecclesia* was written, the last of the ecumenical councils, that of Florence, had been closed for only eight years. Turrecremata lists this Council, together with that of Basle, out of which the Council of Florence grew, as having been called for the fourth of those reasons which he alleges as justifying the summoning of an ecumenical council, namely: "for the bringing back or the confutation, of heretics, by way of disputation." According to the *Summa de ecclesia*:

For this reason in our own days the synod of Basle was convoked for the return of the Bohemians. In this synod the Bohemians were given permission to dispute and to say whatever they wished in defence of their own errors. There were four Catholic teachers assigned to answer them in the public sessions. A long dispute took place, and we were present throughout it. But, although they were very manifestly shown up as being in error, and although a great deal of condescension was shown to them in order that they might be won back, nevertheless they went away with their offences as flagrant as they had been when they arrived. And for the same reason in our days the most widely attended synod of Florence was gathered together by Pope Eugene of holy memory for the return of the Greeks. At this synod there was present the Emperor of the Greeks and the Patriarch of Constantinople, together with many other prelates of the oriental Church. At this gathering, through the work of Our Saviour, who is the true Peace, the wall that divided the Western Church from the Eastern Church was taken away and union and concord were established between the groups, although, alas, the settlement was not accepted by all in the East.[28]

Turrecremata distinguishes between the reasons for calling a general or universal council and the advantages that have been gained by or through such gatherings. "The Utility of the Holding of Councils" is the topic of the tenth chapter in the third book of the *Summa de ecclesia*. And it is quite interesting to see that, in giving examples to prove the various points that he makes, Turrecremata is not at all scrupulous about citing genuine ecumenical councils (which, incidentally he calls universal and

---

[28] *Ibid.*

plenary councils), or even about citing strictly ecclesiastical councils in the proper sense of the term.

First of all, according to the *Summa de ecclesia,* "the holding of universal councils is effective for the conservation of the Christian religion in the unity of the faith, which is the first bond of the Christian society, as the blessed Chrysostom says."[29] And, in the second place, "the holding of these universal councils is worth while for an easier and firmer elucidation of the truth in the midst of doubt." And, as a third advantage to be gained by the holding of universal councils, Turrecremata says that the Lord's field, which is the Church militant of the New Testament, is cultivated by the holding of such assemblies. Through the universal councils, what is good in the Church can be advanced and encouraged, and what is unworthy of the Church and its Divine Founder can be removed most effectively.

The fourth among the advantages which Turrecremata sees as accruing from the holding of an ecumenical council is the crushing of the pride of infidels and tyrants. "As we have heard from those who are considered trustworthy," the author of the *Summa de ecclesia* tells us, "the infidels in the East, that is, in Turkey, are terrified when they learn that universal councils are being held among the Christians, and this happens wherever they may be found, and for a very good reason, since the Church of God, according to the sixth chapter of the Canticle of Canticles, is as terrible as an army set in battle array."[30]

As a fifth advantage to be gained from councils (and very definitely and noticeably Turrecremata does not say, as he says in every other case, that he is dealing with *universal* councils), the author of the *Summa de ecclesia* states that councils are useful "to restrain the enormities of certain bishops who exercise their pontifical office according to their own whim, in violation of the rules of the sacred Fathers, who dishonor their pontificate by simony, or who abuse their pontifical office by worldly vanity or by a scandalous life."[31] And, as the sixth advantage to be gained

[29] *Ibid.,* c. 10.
[30] *Ibid.*
[31] *Ibid.*

from the calling of a general council (and this time he explicitly speaks of general councils), Turrecremata lists the extinction of everything in the line of scandal which comes to arise within the Church.

The *Summa de ecclesia* goes on to say that the personal presence of the Roman pontiff is not required for the validity of a universal council, despite the fact that regularly such councils must be called by his authority, and that such councils must be sustained by him. But it declares that "only bishops or major prelates must necessarily be invited to universal councils."[32] What Turrecremata has to say about others who may be invited to universal or ecumenical councils is thus expressed:

> With reference to the way in which universal councils are to be conducted, especially with regard to those who are to be invited or admitted over and above the bishops, it is to be noted that no certain form has been given. The reason would seem to be that the form and the method of conducting universal councils depends entirely upon the disposition of the Pope, who, by authority and power, is over the universal councils. . . . According to the variety of cases and of affairs the Pope can invite or admit one group or another. Consequently from the manner or the form observed in one universal council or in another, either by the Apostles or by the Fathers who have succeeded them, no effective demonstration can be drawn, since various forms have been observed with reference to people who have been admitted or not admitted as members of the universal councils.[33]

When he asks whether or not all the bishops or the major prelates of the Catholic Church are to be invited to a universal council, Turrecremata falls back on his original distinction between the two kinds of what he calls universal councils. He makes it quite clear that not all the bishops of the world are to be called to a council which is universal merely by reason of the universality of jurisdiction of the man who presides over it. But, with regard to the universal council, which he calls a plenary council, and which is designated as an ecumenical council according to our modern terminology, he has this to say, "For the *per-*

---

[32] *Ibid.,* c. 12.
[33] *Ibid.,* c. 15.

fection all the bishops of the world are to be convoked. If not all are to be called individually, at least all the Patriarchs and the Primates are to be convoked and invited to come with the Bishops they choose to bring with them."[34] Turrecremata states that it is neither possible nor desirable that all the bishops should be gathered together.

As it stands in the *Summa de ecclesia,* the theology of the universal council has definitely a moral aspect. In our time we are accustomed to hear and to speak especially about the power and the authority of the councils and their members. The great theologians of the golden age were also firm on these points, but they likewise spoke of the obligations incumbent upon those who entered into a council which set out to teach and to issue commands in the name of Our Lord. Turrecremata speaks about these qualifications twice, once when he describes the characteristics of those who are called to enter an ecumenical council, and once when he tells of the things the members of the universal council are called upon to avoid.

In the nineteenth chapter of his third book of the *Summa de Ecclesia,* Turrecremata explains that every man called to an ecumenical council should possess these four qualities: wisdom, holiness, experience, and zeal for the Church.[35] Quite obviously these characteristics should be found in any man chosen for a position which would qualify him for membership in an ecumenical council. And, as the text of the chapter stands, it is also quite evident that, according to the mind of this great theologian, these are likewise qualities which the men called to the council should take care to develop within themselves so that they may become operative during the course of these most important of ecclesiastical gatherings.

In the context of the *Summa de ecclesia* it is quite evident that the *sapientia* or wisdom to which the author refers as a requisite characteristic of a man who is called upon to take an effective part in a universal council is an accurate and profound grasp of

---

[34] *Ibid.,* c. 16.
[35] This is connected with Turrecremata's contention that not every "major prelate" should necessarily be invited to an ecumenical council.

the truths of sacred theology, which is the *sapientia* governing all the other studies attainable by man.[36] Turrecremata points to the fact that it ill becomes a man to set out to expound the Church's doctrine to others unless he himself is most perfectly versed in this same body of truth.

Furthermore, since the purpose of the council, which is the purpose of the government of the Church itself, is and must always be the increase of sanctity within the people of God, a man who has no care for that objective is ill fitted to assume a place within the universal council.[37] However, the author insists that the men called to the council must be those who have experience within their own field. They are supposed to be working for the good of souls, within the framework of the apostolic activity of the Catholic priesthood. Then, logically, according to Turrecremata, they should be men who are accustomed to work for the good of souls within this area. They should know the needs that they are expected to satisfy, and they should know how these needs are to be met. The universal council is definitely not a place in which men should gain their first experience in the field of apostolic endeavor.

Finally, the man who is called to the universal council to work as a member of this gathering should have the zeal for the house of God which is the Church militant of the New Testament. The great good to which the council is ordered is the betterment of the Church of God in this world. It is quite obvious that, if a man is not intensely interested in the attainment of this objective, he will be a hindrance rather than a help as a part of an ecumenical council.

This is what Turrecremata has to say about the qualities that should be possessed by any prelate who is invited to take part in a general council. Along this same line, and still more interesting to a twentieth-century student, is the list of offences which those called to the council should seek to avoid, "if," in the language of Turrecremata, "they want to have their synod venerated by the

---

[36] Cf. *Summa de ecclesia,* c. 19.
[37] Cf. *ibid.*

world and by the Church and useful to both." The author of the *Summa de ecclesia* lists twelve of these faults.[38]

(1) The first of these is malice or perversity of affection. Thus, according to Turrecremata, "all sinister and evil talk must be banished far from the Fathers who are gathering for a council, and their entire intention must be directed towards God's honor and glory."

In other words, the man who enters a council of the Catholic Church, like a man who goes out to say Mass or to receive the Holy Eucharist, must be in the state of grace, actually loving God with a supernatural affection enlightened by divine faith. Turrecremata sees three reasons that necessitate this conclusion.

(A) There is no third status between the state of grace, which necessarily involves divine charity, and the status of sin or aversion from God. Thus the man who goes into the council without true and supernatural charity is actually entering into this gathering in a condition of opposition to Christ, like the members of the council of the chief priests and the elders that St. Matthew describes as being called together against Our Lord.

(B) The men who enter into a council as members are performing an apostolic work. They obviously have need of apostolic holiness. They are obligated to keep up the apostolic dignity and to guard the authority of the apostles.

(C) A council is meant to bring peace and security to the Church. The man who enters this council in a state of aversion from God will tend to act against these objectives. Turrecremata takes cognizance of the fact that "the assistance of Christ's divinity is promised to those who are gathered together in truth and in the name of Christ."

(2) The Fathers of the council must see to it that there is no neglect of the common good. They must work with all their strength for the benefit of the Church as a whole, passing over their own private or individual advantage.

(3) The third thing which the Fathers of the council are bound in conscience to avoid is timidity. No one should be afraid to tell the truth about what he actually thinks on subjects

---

[38] Cf. *ibid.*, c. 27.

that pertain to God's glory and the beauty of His House, which is the Catholic Church.

(4) The fourth fault which the Fathers of the council must avoid is, according to the author of the *Summa de ecclesia,* vanity or vain glory. He, with his own wide experience in conciliar activity, knew very well that there would always be a temptation for some of the Fathers of the council to use this gathering as a forum to show off what they regarded as their own intellectual gifts, and thus to waste the time and effort that should be devoted to a firm statement of the Christian faith and to the prudent and effective guidance of God's people.

(5) Turrecremata, who was well aware of what went on in the councils of his own era, since he was one of the most important personalities at Basle and at Florence, pointed out another fault that must be avoided by the Fathers if the conciliar gathering is to be successful for the cause of Christ's truth and justice. The Fathers must not indulge in too much feasting. The spirit of a council called for the well-being of Our Lord's Church should be as far as possible removed from the spirit of the carnival or the banquet hall.

(6) Still more to be avoided by the Fathers of a council is the spirit of obstinate dispute and dissension. This, more than any other, is the factor which can wreck the deliberations of an ecclesiastical gathering. The men who are called to such a gathering are expected to testify to the unity of Catholic belief, rather than to uphold any opinions which may, in one way or another, have become attached to their names.

(7) The seventh of these faults which must be avoided by any man who is called upon to take part in an ecumenical council is described by Turrecremata as *Tepida correctio circa culpas praeteritas et maxime in domo Domini commissas.* In explaining the meaning of this offence, the author of the *Summa de ecclesia* appeals to the laxity of the priest Heli, who condoned or at least did nothing to punish or counteract the sins committed by his sons, and the zeal for the house of God that was shown by Our Lord when He cast the money changers out of the temple.

(8) The eighth of these faults which, according to Turrecremata, must be avoided by any man who wishes to enter in a
worthy manner into the deliberation of an ecumenical council is
hatred, in virtue of which a man might try to employ the council
as an instrument in working off his own grudges. This, of course,
is one of the fundamental laws in all of the theology of the
universal council.

Far more perfectly than the men of our own time, the theologians of the golden age realized that the primary responsibility
incumbent upon the members of the true Church was that of
obeying the divine command that we should love one another.
Throughout the Gospel according to St. John, and throughout the
First Epistle of St. John, which, in the last analysis, is a sort of
covering letter for the fourth Gospel, we run across that command,
that we should love one another, that the follower of Christ was
in duty-bound to forgive his brother from his heart, and that, if
a man's brother, that is, his fellow disciple or his fellow member
of the society of the disciples, had anything against him, the
offender was to leave his sacrifice before the altar and go and be
reconciled with his brother. Turrecremata was realistic enough
to know that men cannot properly teach and legislate in the name
of Our Lord unless they took care to carry out this most important
of Our Lord's commands in their own lives.

(9) The ninth of these observations made by the author of
the *Summa de ecclesia* is most interesting. The Fathers of the
ecclesiastical council are to see to it that they do not allow their
ordinances to be based on "any fantasies, or dreams, or uncertain
revelations, or visions," but they are to be guided solely by the
rules of the sacred letters, that is, of genuine divine public revelation. The fact that someone may claim that some private revelation or some vision might militate in favor of a certain course of
action must not be allowed to influence men who are being called
upon to exercise apostolic activity within the true Church of
Christ.

(10) Turrecremata insists that the Fathers in any ecclesiastical
council must avoid this error. They must not reverse the divinely
imposed order in the Church by setting temporal things ahead of

the spiritual goods which the council is summoned to procure for the people of God. The spiritual goods, to which every other consideration must be subordinated, are the blessings pertaining to the Christian faith, to divine worship, to the reformation of morals, and to the peace of the Christian populace.

(11) Again, Turrecremata insists that the Fathers of the council are obligated in conscience to see to it that there is no precipitateness or lack of care in their deliberations. The seriousness of the material they have met to discuss and to decide upon makes it imperative that all care should be given to the decision of the council.

(12) Finally, the Fathers of the council are obligated in conscience to see to it that there is no impairment of freedom of decision in the council. By its very essence the ecclesiastical council is a gathering in which the members of the hierarchy, or, as Turrecremata puts it, the "major prelates of the Catholic Church," freely govern and teach the Church militant of the New Testament. Any undue influence or violence practiced against the Fathers of the council will be such as to hurt the work of the council. Turrecremata points to the Robber Synod of Ephesus, held in 449, as a gathering which was rendered inoperative by reason of a lack of freedom.

Again, Turrecremata was convinced that any major prelate who was invited to take part in a universal ecclesiastical council could not in conscience refuse to attend this meeting unless, for reasons of health or for some other very serious cause, such attendance was impossible. And the civil rulers who impeded the holding of an ecclesiastical council were to be considered as tyrants and as enemies of God's Church.

One of the most interesting sections of the theology of the universal council, as this is found in Turrecremata's *Summa de ecclesia,* is the part having to do with the relations between the Roman pontiff and the universal council. First of all, he pointed out that regularly the Roman pontiff was to preside at such a council, either in person or through his delegates. Furthermore, he held, following the lead of St. Thomas Aquinas, that the authority of the council universally depends upon and emanates from the Roman pontiff. It was his teaching that the universal, or as we would say the ecumenical, council derived its authority from Our Lord through the Roman pontiff, and he believed that this doctrine was not merely certain but a dogma of the Catholic faith.[39]

Furthermore, it was the contention of Turrecremata that whatever was established, defined, or stated in a universal council was established, defined, and stated by the Roman pontiff as a principal cause. And he spoke of the laudable custom of ancient councils by which these gatherings did not issue any definitions pertaining to faith except where the Roman pontiff had previously settled that question in what we would now call the course of his ordinary teaching activity.[40] As a theologian he knew that the decrees of a general council needed to be confirmed and promulgated by the sovereign pontiff.

Likewise a part of the theology of the ecumenical council, in the *Summa de ecclesia* of John de Turrecremata, is the teaching that the jurisdiction of the pope is such that under no circumstances can there be an appeal from the decision of a pope to that of a council. Thus he showed that the jurisdiction of the Roman pontiff is, in the last analysis, superior to that of a council. And, like all the other theologians of his era, Turrecremata stated that the council could never have any jurisdiction over a true pope except in a case in which the pope himself had fallen into public heresy, and had thus forfeited his membership in the Church.

Another conclusion with reference to the relations between the Roman pontiff and the universal council of the Catholic Church is the statement that the Roman pontiff cannot subject himself to the decisions of a universal council. Likewise, according to this first complete theological treatise on the universal councils, these gatherings cannot invalidate the decrees of the Roman pontiff. But, on the other hand, this same book teaches that the Roman pontiff can dispense from laws passed by a universal council, and that one pope can certainly remove statutes (although obviously not doctrinal definitions) made by his predecessors.

---

[39] Cf. *ibid.,* c. 28.
[40] Cf. *ibid.,* c. 33.

The crowning point of Turrecremata's treatise on the universal councils is his thesis to the effect that with regard to things which have been defined by the unanimous agreement of the Fathers and of the Roman pontiff, a universal council cannot err in matters relating to the faith. At the same time, however, Turrecremata taught that, without the agreement and the consent of the Pope, a gathering of bishops which otherwise might have been a universal council of the Catholic Church could fall into error on matters relating to the divine and Catholic faith. A tremendous amount of documentation, most of it, like most of the other material in the *Summa de ecclesia,* derived from the content of the *Corpus iuris canonici,* backs up Turrecremata's thesis.[41] But we must not allow ourselves to forget that it is a thesis which was demonstrated in a very practical way during the course of Turrecremata's lifetime by the councils of Constance and Basle.

At this point, towards the end of his treatise, Turrecremata took cognizance of an objection brought up from within the membership of the Church against the infallibility of the universal council. The objectors pointed to the fact that, during the course of Our Lord's passion, and up until the time of His resurrection, the apostles themselves had all sinned against the faith. Thus, they argued, the apostolic college, which is made up of the Pope and the residential bishops of the Catholic Church, can likewise fail in matters of divine faith.

Turrecremata answered that, at this particular time, St. Peter had been promised, but had not actually been given, the position of pastor of the universal Church. Furthermore, he pointed to the fact that, in that particular period, the other apostles were not yet in charge of souls. And here he took the opportunity to state again a thesis dear to many of the great theologians of the golden age, to the effect that, during the time of Our Lord's passion and death, the Blessed Virgin alone maintained the faith which was the acceptance of the divinely revealed message[42] Our Lord had delivered to His disciples. It was his contention, and he demonstrated the truth of his assertion, that this fall of the

---

[41] Cf. *ibid.,* c. 58.
[42] Cf. *ibid.,* c. 61.

apostolic college, along with its leader, in no way involved or implied the possibility of fallibility on matters of the faith on the part of the apostolic college after Our Lord's ascension into heaven.

Furthermore, in the treatise of Turrecremata, if a council should prove to be contumacious, and to act against the teachings of the faith, or to proceed in one way or another against the best interests of the Catholic people, it was well within the competence of the Roman pontiff to correct, to condemn, or to dissolve such an assembly. In other words, Turrecremata definitely did not believe that the Roman pontiff was obliged to give an automatic approval to any universal assembly of the major prelates of the Catholic Church, even to an assembly which he himself had called as a universal council.[43]

With the experience of the councils of Pisa, Constance, and Basle behind them, the men of Turrecremata's day were apt to ask about what was to be done in the event that the decrees of one council ran counter to that of another. Restricting his answer to the case of the universal council, the author of the *Summa de ecclesia* set forth these principles:[44]

(1) Where there are two genuine universal councils, both of which are legitimate and approved by the Roman See, there is no possibility of any contradiction between them in matters of faith.

(2) Where there is a difference in terminology, it is essential that the meaning set forth in the earlier of these two legitimate and genuine universal councils should not be represented as having been modified or corrected by the later gathering. The teaching of the *Summa de ecclesia* on this point is the very truth which was so powerfully stressed in the Vatican Council's constitution, *Dei Filius,* and in the Oath against Modernism, incorporated into the *Sacrorum antistitum.*

(3) Where laws passed or enacted by a later council differ from precepts imposed by a former assembly, those of the more recent council are to be followed.

---

[43] Cf. *ibid.,* c. 62.
[44] Cf. *ibid.,* c. 63.

Turrecremata also envisions the possibility of a council at which the pope is opposed by the other bishops. This will not happen with regard to matters of faith, if the council is a legitimate universal council. But even where it is a matter of interpretation of law, the control always belongs to the Vicar of Christ, the only one who is commissioned directly by Our Lord to act as the pastor of His universal Church militant. Where the members of a council differ on a question which is being put forward as a matter of faith, Turrecremata makes this distinction:

(A) Where the question is clear cut, and it is obvious from the sources of the faith and from the literature of Catholic theology that one of the answers is the correct one, then a man would be obligated in conscience to hold out for this answer, even when the vast majority of the assembly was opposed to him. The author of the *Summa de ecclesia* cites the examples of the Robber Synod of Ephesus (449) and the Council of Ariminum (359) to show that those who sided with the majority in these assemblies, even before they were rejected by the Roman See, were guilty of sins against the faith.

(B) Where there is not this absolutely preponderant evidence, it can be assumed that the majority is correct, and, in any given situation of this kind, a member of the council could regularly assume that the majority was right.

Finally the *Summa de ecclesia* finishes its treatise on the universal council with the observations that the Roman pontiff can, if he deems it right or necessary, transfer a council from one place to another, and can likewise dissolve a council, even when the members of the council wish to have it continue.

Such, briefly, is the content of the treatise on the universal councils in the first theological work which could be called a relatively complete exposition of ecclesiology. The author was a scholastic theologian, but the work itself was not then a part of scholastic theology. It was primarily controversial or polemical theology, and the sources used throughout the work, and particularly in the treatise on the universal councils, were pre-eminently those taken from the *Corpus iuris canonici*. The scholastic treatise on the councils, when this section was introduced into the framework of scholastic theology towards the beginning of the seventeenth century, was substantially the collection of theses set forth in the *Summa de ecclesia.* It is true that there were refinements in some of the theses. It is also true that, during the years after Turrecremata had written, in the years when this treatise on the councils was receiving its final polishing, the *Corpus iuris canonici* was no longer used as the most important source in support of these theses. But, compared with the material in the first book of the *Summa de ecclesia,* the doctrine dealing with the Church as a whole, the material of the third book, that dealing with the universal councils, underwent very little change in content or in direction.

Actually, however, as the treatise on the councils entered into the fabric of scholastic theology, it came from the *Controversies* of St. Robert Bellarmine rather than from the *Summa de ecclesia* of Turrecremata. As a matter of fact, the first two books in the Controversies *De Conciliis et Ecclesia* deal with the theology of the councils. The first explains the nature and the functioning of the universal council, while the second has to do with its authority in the Church of God. Incidentally, the famous book *De ecclesia militante* is the third of the books that go to make up the Controversies *De Conciliis et Ecclesia,* while the treatise *De notis ecclesiae* constitutes the fourth of these books.

St. Robert Bellarmine added very little to what we might call the substance of the theology of the ecumenical councils. But he certainly put the material into much better theological arrangement than had his great predecessor in this field. His proofs are more cogent, and certainly less dependent on the literature of canon law. The wording of his theses is sometimes more precise, or at least more effective.

One of St. Robert's great contributions to the theology of the ecumenical council was his thesis, which he presents merely as more probable teaching, that the councils are in the Church by reason of the divine constitution of the Church itself.[45] He

---

[45] "*Hanc autem originem Conciliorum, etsi Albertus Pighius . . . contendat esse plane humanam et naturali ratione excogitatam, probabilius tamen est, divinam esse*" (*De conciliis et ecclesia,* Lib. I, *De Conciliis,* c. 3).

pointed to the fact that official acts of ecumenical councils had asserted that Our Lord's words, recorded in the eighteenth chapter of the Gospel according to St. Matthew, "For where there are two or three gathered together in my name, there am I in the midst of them,"[46] constituted a divine promise of assistance for conciliar action within the true Church. And it was likewise the contention of St. Robert that the apostles would never have said, "For it hath seemed good to the Holy Ghost and to us,"[47] in their letter giving the decrees of the Council of Jerusalem, if there were no direct divine sanction for conciliar action within the Church.

Another very important advance made in the *Controversies* was the listing of the ecumenical councils substantially in the way they are set down today in the literature of sacred theology. Turrecremata had numbered only the eight ecumenical councils held in the East. He did not assign any special numbers to the councils in the West. Indeed, with his distinction between the two different kinds of universal councils, the ones which were universal merely by reason of the universal authority of the one who presided over them, and those which were universal in that they were attended by the major prelates of the Catholic Church from all parts of the world, his teaching on the ecumenical councils of the West was inclined to lose some of its clarity. St. Robert, on the other hand, explained the list of the true ecumenical councils (he called them general councils) much more effectively than they are explained in most of the current theological literature.

St. Robert spoke of four different kinds of general councils. The first group included those which were approved. There were eighteen on that list, the eight councils held in the East, and the general or ecumenical councils of the West from the First Lateran in 1123 until the Council of Trent, which was, for him, the most recent of the general councils. In this list he did not include the Council of Constance.[48] It is interesting to note that, writing almost fifty years after the publication of St. Robert's *Contro-*

---

[46] *Matt.*, 18:20.
[47] *Acts*, 15:28.
[48] Cf. St. Robert, *De Conciliis et Ecclesia*, Lib. I, c. 5.

versies, the great Francis Sylvius of Douai used this same division and did not include the Council of Constance in his list of general councils approved by the Holy See.[49] And, for that matter, Froget, writing in the DTC, does not count Constance as one of the true ecumenical councils.[50]

The second group of general councils listed by St. Robert was that of councils called as general councils but rejected as such by the Roman See. He included eight of these gatherings in this list. The first three of these were councils dominated by the Arians during the course of the fourth century. The fourth was the Robber Synod of Ephesus. The fifth and sixth were iconoclastic gatherings. The seventh was a council assembled at Pisa against Julius II, a gathering repudiated and condemned by the Fifth Council of the Lateran. The eighth was a gathering of Lutheran pastors at Wittenberg, a gathering which, in St. Robert's time, the Lutherans described as a general council.

The third group of councils which St. Robert listed as general, partly approved and in part repudiated and rejected, was made up of eight of these assemblies. The first of these was the Council of Sardica, which was held in 351. For many years the canons of this council were mistakenly considered enactments by the Council of Nicea in the western world. The others were the Council of Sirmium, in 356, the Trullan or Quinisext Council of Constantinople, in 692, the Council of Frankfurt, in 794, the Council of Constance, 1414-1418, and finally the Council of Basle, which began in 1431.

It is interesting to note that St. Robert considered the antipope elected at Pisa, Alexander V, and his successor, John XXIII, as having been probably true popes. He considered that teaching a *communis opinio.* Sylvius agrees with St. Robert at least as far as the legitimacy of the election of Alexander is concerned. Both of them based their contention in great measure on the fact that the next indubitably genuine pontiff to take the name Alexander called himself Alexander VI, thereby seeming at least to concede

---

[49] Cf. Sylvius, *op. cit.,* Lib. IV, q. 1, art. 4.

[50] Cf. *Dictionnaire de théologie catholique,* III, col. 673, where Froget classifies Constance as approved in part and not approved in part.

the legitimacy of the election of Alexander V. But it is interesting to note that the next true pope who took the name John calls himself John XXIII, thereby showing that the John XXIII who succeeded Alexander, the man elected at the Council of Pisa, was an antipope rather than a true Roman pontiff.

In point of fact, of course, the conduct of Alexander VI in this regard proved absolutely nothing. Even the most elementary study of the list of the popes will show that many a pope has taken a number one above that claimed by a previous antipope merely for the sake of avoiding confusion.

Where Turrecremata had listed twelve causes which made the calling of an ecumenical council useful, St. Robert Bellarmine enumerated six of these motives. They were:

(1) A new heresy, new in the sense that it had not yet been condemned by the universal Church (It was St. Robert's contention that "the Church always considers new heresies to be so dangerous that it thinks that the only way in which they can be resisted is by having all or at least a great number of the princes of the Church join forces to present a united front in battling against the enemies of the faith."[51] Like Turrecremata, upon whom he obviously depends, St. Robert asserts that the first seven general councils were called for this purpose.);

(2) A schism among Roman pontiffs, that is, a situation in which two or more men, who had to be taken seriously, claimed the dignity and the responsibility of the papal office (St. Robert lists the councils of Pisa and of Constance as having been called for this reason.);

(3) The common or united resistance of the Church to some enemy of the Church (St. Robert lists the First Lateran Council [1123] among the councils called for this purpose. In this case the common enemy of the Church was the Saracen military power.);

(4) The suspicion of heresy in the Roman pontiff"[52] (Once again it must be noted that neither St. Robert nor the other great theologians like Sylvius who accepted his teaching could ever

[51] St. Robert, *op. cit.*, Lib. I, c. 9.
[52] *Ibid.*

envision the possibility that a Roman pontiff could teach heresy when he was speaking *ex cathedra*. And furthermore, by reason of their theological principles, as well as by reason of their command of history, these men never thought of a genuine ecumenical council being called for this purpose.);

(5) A serious doubt about the legitimacy or the validity of the election of a Roman pontiff;

(6) The general reformation of abuses and vices which have crept into the Church (St. Robert admits that the Roman pontiff can legislate for the entire Church of God by himself, without calling a general council. But at the same time he takes cognizance of the fact that, if he legislates along with an ecumenical council, his rulings may prove to be more effective.).

After taking all these facts into consideration, St. Robert arrived at the following conclusion: "I say this about general councils; that the calling of such councils is most useful, and sometimes in a certain sense necessary, but that such convocation is never *simpliciter* and absolutely necessary."[53] But, in a general way, he holds that councils of some sort are absolutely necessary for the Church, since conciliar activity is a part of the divinely constituted operation of Christ's kingdom on earth according to the dispensation of the New Testament.

In accordance with the principles of scholastic ecclesiology St. Robert insisted on what is now and always has been a truth of this science: that it is within the competence of the Roman pontiff alone to call a general council of the Catholic Church. He taught that in cases where there was some question about the identity of the true pope, a council which was definitely not a perfect and complete general council, a council which could not issue infallible definitions about matters concerning the faith, could be brought into being with the consent of the cardinals or the bishops.

When he comes to discuss the men who are to be called to a general or ecumenical council, St. Robert gives this as the *"sententia catholicorum."* It is the same conclusion which is taught in the schools today.

---

[53] *Ibid.*, c. 10.

All and only the major prelates, that is, the bishops, ordinarily have the right of a decisive vote in general or in provincial councils. Nevertheless, out of privilege and custom, cardinals, abbots, and generals of orders, even though they are not bishops, have that same right. From among the priests and the other minor clerics there are called only certain learned men who may help in the discussions or in the service of the gathering. Princes also may be called both so that they may defend the council and so that they may be witnesses to what the council is doing and aware of what is going on, in order that later they may penalize individuals who contumaciously disobey the decrees of the council.[54]

It is quite interesting to see the way in which St. Robert, as a theologian, handles the question as to how many bishops must be present at a gathering in order that this gathering may be considered as an ecumenical or general council. He begins his consideration of this question with the remark that here we must be guided entirely by the tradition and the custom of the Catholic Church. And from this custom he finds that four principles emerge as valid in this area.

(1) The invitation to the council must be general, so that it is known to all the major regions where the Christian Church exists.

(2) No one who actually comes to the council is to be excluded as long as it is obvious that he really is a bishop and in good standing. Here it is interesting to note that neither St. Robert nor any of the other ecclesiologists of the golden age ever took cognizance of the difference between a residential bishop and what is now known as a titular bishop, that is, a man who has episcopal orders, but who has no existent local church which he is to govern as a pastor and a father. Where the men of this era speak of the bishops of the Catholic Church, it seems to be understood that they are dealing only with residential bishops.

(3) In order that there should be a general council of the Catholic Church it was regularly or ordinarily requisite that there should be present, either personally, or at least by representation,

---

[54] *Ibid.*, c. 15

bishops from all the major patriarchates of the world. Thus, apart from the Roman patriarchate, the patriarchate of the West, there should also be represented regularly the four great patriarchates of the Orient, those of Constantinople, Alexandria, Antioch, and Jerusalem. But, as St. Robert teaches, in line with what had been taught by Turrecremata before him, it is not now necessary to have these patriarchs represented, since they are heretical or certainly at least schismatic.

(4) Finally, it is requisite that some at least should come from most of the parts of the Church. St. Robert takes cognizance of the fact that there were no representatives from the Western Church present at either the First Ecumenical Council of Constantinople or at the Council of Ephesus, but he remarks that these councils were approved as ecumenical by the Roman See.

St. Robert teaches insistently that the bishops who are members of a general council act as judges, and not merely as counsellors to the pope. At the same time, however, he brings out the fact that it is within the right and the competence of the Roman pontiff alone to preside at a general council, either personally or through his representatives.

In concluding his first book, the one on the nature of the general councils, St. Robert considers the conditions which the Protestants of his time attached to their attendance at any general council. It was the desire of the Church that they should come and re-enter Catholic unity, but they said that they would do so only if the following conditions were met:

(1) All the decrees of the Council of Trent were to be declared invalid;

(2) The council was to be held in Germany;

(3) The Roman pontiff should not convoke the council nor should he preside over it; instead he was to be treated as one of the parties in litigation;

(4) The decisions were to be reached using scripture as the only norm, and not considering tradition or the canons;

(5) The decisions of this gathering were to be arrived at, not by any majority of votes, but simply in terms of the conformity of the judgments with the word of God;

(6) The Roman pontiff was to release all prelates from the oaths of fidelity to him;

(7) The theologians of the princes and the states which adhered to the confession of Augsburg should have the same position in this council as that given to bishops;

(8) There should be guaranteed not only the safe conduct of individuals, but also the formulas of belief set forth by the Lutherans should be guaranteed against condemnation on the part of the Catholic prelates.[55]

The only element in this series of conditions which St. Robert found acceptable was that there should be safe conduct given to individuals who would see fit to attend any general council.

The second of the books in the general controversy *De Conciliis et Ecclesia* is the one, *De conciliorum auctoritate.* The main thesis of this book is the statement: "It must be held as a dogma of the Catholic faith that general councils which have been approved by the Sovereign Pontiff can err neither in faith nor in morals."[56] In the manner which has become classical in scholastic theology, but which not all theologians have followed as well as St. Robert, the author of the *Controversies* then sets out to prove his thesis from scripture, from the Fathers, and from reason.

He likewise states and proves the thesis that particular councils which have been approved by the sovereign pontiff can err neither in faith nor in morals. Here he answers objections set forth in the name of scripture, of the Fathers, of Church history, and of reason.

St. Robert teaches also as valid theological conclusions that particular councils cannot be taken as infallible if they have not been approved by the Roman pontiff, and that even general councils are definitely fallible if their teaching be considered before the confirmation by the pope, or as given apart from his instructions. He insists, in line with the dictates of the Catholic faith, that the Roman pontiff is really above the council, since the Roman pontiff is by divine commission the visible head of the entire Catholic Church. He is, to quote the teaching of St.

---

[55] Cf. *ibid.,* c. 21.

[56] *De conciliis et ecclesia,* Lib. II, *De conciliorum auctoritate,* c. 1.

Robert, which was defined in the First Vatican Council, "the pastor and the head, not only of all the individual churches, but also of the entire universal Church taken together. He has been constituted as such by Our Lord Himself."

And, on the other hand, "the supreme power over the Church is not in the Church itself nor in any council apart from the Pope," either formally as such or radically, in the sense that the power in a state is always radically within the people who are governed.

The sovereign pontiff cannot allow either a council or any individual or group of individuals within the Church to judge him, that is, to act as an authority superior to him within the Church of God.

This is the content of the theology of the general council, as it is found in the writings of St. Robert Bellarmine and Francis Sylvius. The teaching has not changed during the course of the centuries. It will not change.

Definitely our knowledge of this teaching will advance and should advance. We would seek to understand better why the Holy Ghost guarantees the infallibility of a general or ecumenical council which has been confirmed by the Roman pontiff. We should seek to understand how and why the general or ecumenical council can legislate for the universal Church in such a way that this council can say as did the apostolic council of Jerusalem, "It has seemed good to the Holy Ghost and to us."[57]

Ultimately the theology of the universal council will embrace a better understanding of the relations between the Roman pontiff and the other bishops within the Catholic Church. And most certainly it will bring out the responsibility and dignity of the teaching office within the Church militant of the New Testament.

Joseph Clifford Fenton

---

[57] *Acts*, 15:28.